Authentic Success

A GUIDE FOR AMBITIOUS WOMEN TO BUILD ALIGNED CAREERS AND LIVES

Kate Rosenberg

Shattered Glass Coaching

Authentic Success:
A Guide For Ambitious Women to Build Aligned Careers and Lives
by Kate Rosenberg

Paperback: 978-1-968960-07-0
Ebook: 978-1-968960-08-7

Library of Congress Control Number: [insert]

Cover Design by Andrew Magee
Printed in the United States of America

Upword Publishing
Denver, CO
upwordpublishing.com

First Edition

Dedication

To every woman who has ever felt stuck, undervalued, or unsure of her next move— this book is for you. Your authentic success is waiting.

Foreword

When I think about the powerful women who have been in my world, whether in business, career, or life, there is a common thread. They are smart, capable, driven, and deeply committed, but they are also tired. Tired of holding it all together, striving for someone else's version of success, or feeling like no matter how much they do, it's never quite enough.

We are living in a time of extraordinary pressure. While we may not enjoy admitting it, deep down we all feel it. Many women are raising families while climbing corporate ladders, building businesses while putting themselves last, and showing up as the "good girl" even when things feel like a shit show on the inside. Our systems are overloaded, and it's no wonder anxiety and guilt have become our daily best friends. Somewhere along the way, getting stuff done has replaced our inner wisdom, and performance has replaced presence.

This is why this book and Kate's voice matter.

I first met Kate when she hired me as her business coach, fresh out of coaching school and ready to build something of her own. I've coached thousands of entrepreneurs and seen so many show up, bright eyed and bushy tailed, believing being a business owner will solve all their problems. Then, it gets real, and most of them fall off or give up. There's a reason over half of all businesses fail within the first 5 years.

Kate, however, was different. Unlike so many, she was willing to do the work. She showed up with passion, honesty, and a rare willingness to look at herself without excuses. Even when she was afraid, she kept going.

As her business got off the ground and started growing, so did my respect for her. I loved working with her so much I eventually invited her to join our coaching team. I supported her continuing to build her own business alongside her coaching role with us, and over the years I've had the privilege and pleasure of watching her live the very principles she now teaches other women.

I've seen her struggle with her own health challenges while building a meaningful business, and move through major life transitions with grace, integrity and self-trust. Kate doesn't just teach this work, she lives it.

What makes Kate unique is not being perfect or polished, or even her endearing "hey ya'll!" It's her openness, vulnerability, and her deep respect for the inner life of the women she serves. She understands clarity doesn't come from more noise or productivity hacks, but from slowing down long enough to hear yourself. This book is not fluffy. It won't tell you who to be or what to want. Instead, she invites you to get honest about your values, habits, how you communicate, and how you define success on your **own** terms.

Kate understands something essential that people many miss. No matter how capable you are, it's nearly impossible to see everything on your own. Having a trusted mentor or outside perspective isn't a weakness; it's a form of self-respect. This book honors that wisdom.

If you are a woman in business or corporate who believes there must be another way to live and succeed that doesn't require you to betray yourself on a daily basis, this book is for you. Read it slowly. Let it challenge you without any judgement or criticism. Let it help you remember who you are beneath the roles, expectations, and noise.

Remember, claiming your worth does not take anything away from anyone else. It simply gives you permission to live more authentically. It's also incredibly freeing to choose yourself while allowing others to do the same.

I'm honored to hand you over to Kate now and trust you're in very good hands.

Jennifer Dawn

Soul-Aligned Business Coach & *Happy Productive Podcast* Host
https://jenniferdawncoaching.com/

Words of Praise/ Endorsements

"Authentic Success is the new blueprint for building success on your terms. Look out- Brené Brown now has a new successor!"

–Jeffrey Hayzlett

C-SUITE NETWORK™ Chairman & Founder
https://c-suitenetwork.com/

"I've already told several people about this book because I know so many will benefit from it. Kate's writing is phenomenal, the exercises are unlike anything I've seen, and her authentic voice shines through every page."

–Jen Schwytzer

LCSW, Speaker & Trainer
https://www.jenschwytzer.com

"Having worked alongside Kate for the past five years as a fellow coach, I've witnessed firsthand how her strategies transform lives—not just in theory, but in practice. Her approach combines real-world insight with actionable frameworks that create lasting change. In *Authentic Success*, Kate provides exactly what ambitious professionals need: a clear, step-by-step process to align their values with their vision. Rather than approaching success from a place of fear or comparison, she shows readers how to rewrite limiting narratives and build empowering ones—with concrete exercises that push beyond what we initially believe possible. These aren't just concepts; they're the same proven methods I've seen produce remarkable results for her clients time and again."

–Julie Moses Whittingham

Life Design Coach, A Life You Love
https://www.alifeyoulove.me/

"If you are a woman in business or corporate who believes there must be another way to live and succeed that doesn't require you to betray yourself on a daily basis, this book is for you. Kate doesn't just teach this work, she lives it—and she invites you to get honest about your values and define success on your own terms."

–Jennifer Dawn

Founder, Jennifer Dawn Coaching
Soul-Aligned Business Coach & *Happy Productive Podcast* Host
https://jenniferdawncoaching.com/

"What I love about *Authentic Success* is how deeply personalized it feels. Kate helps you clarify who you are, what you believe, and the concrete steps to elevate not just your career, but your whole life. With warmth, honesty, and light personal stories, she guides you the way a truly supportive parent or mentor would: steady, affirming, and real."

–Carlyn Wice

Human Resources Consultant, Carlyn Carter Consulting
https://carlyncarterconsulting.com/

"Kate's authenticity shines through every page, and her examples and anecdotes really solidify her points. This book is personable, credible, and full of actionable wisdom for anyone ready to define success on their own terms."

–Douglas Robbins

Best-Selling Author, Podcast Host, and Writing Coach
https://douglasrobbinsauthor.com/

Table of Contents

Introduction

Success [sək-ˈses] (noun): a favorable or desired outcome
There are books out there that claim a "proven method" for achieving success if you simply follow the steps. Others provide a so-called playbook for women to climb to the top of the corporate ladder in a male-dominated world.

This book is not that type of one-size-fits-all guide.

This is a program for career success that focuses on blazing a path to fulfillment and prosperity that is authentic to YOU. My name is Kate Rosenberg, and I'll be your coach on the journey to discovering your authentic success. Through these pages, I will provide you with guidance, support, and accountability, which is exactly what I do for my career coaching clients in my day-to-day work.

The reality is that success is defined subjectively. For one person, it can be making $1 million a year and traveling on luxurious vacations every month. For another person, success may be earning a modest salary, living frugally, and simply in nature.

I can't give you a proven step-by-step process, because I don't know what success means to you. This book is about guiding you to answer that question for yourself. And if you're not sure what it means yet, you're in the right place.

Authentic success is about getting your desired outcome in a way that feels genuine and aligned with you—your values, goals, and happiness.

At the start of my program, many of the women I coach aren't clear on their goals and aren't even sure what their "desired outcome" is. Fewer than 50 percent of them even know where they want to be in 10 years. A 45-year-old tech executive hired me as her coach after saying, "I want you to help me figure out what I want to be when I grow up." Of my clients who <u>are</u> crystal clear about what they want, many aren't sure how to get there. They don't know where to start or how to achieve their desired results.

The first step on your journey is gaining clarity on your goals and desired outcomes. Achieving that success depends entirely on what you want the process to look like and feel like. There are many paths to achieve success, and you can choose the route that is authentic for you.

But here's what I do know:

You **don't** have to be calculating or unkind to climb your way to the top of the corporate ladder.

You **don't** have to keep your mouth shut and go along with what everyone else is saying out of fear of conflict or confrontation.

The women I coach have many different personalities, communication styles, and ways to handle challenges. But the women who are MOST successful have this in common: They embrace their authentic personality, values, and natural behaviors as a guiding star on their path to success. They're not pretending to be someone else or living a lie about success that they've been sold by society.

Faking it isn't really making it. You can't be someone you're not. That comes across as phony, which people can smell from a mile away.

Authentic success is knowing who you are at your core, including your strengths, weaknesses, values, beliefs, and long-term goals, and acting in a way that is aligned.

You **don't** need to change your personality or bend over backward to get a promotion.

You **don't** need to be a doormat to be a good wife or friend.

You **certainly don't** need to compromise your values to make millions of dollars.

Anything you want to achieve, personally or professionally, is possible just by being authentically *you*.

This book is a tool, guiding you toward achieving authentic success. It follows the same structure as that which I take my coaching clients through, with guided exercises and a clearly stated goal. At the end of each chapter, you'll find exercises to complete. I strongly recommend sitting down with a pen and paper or your laptop and actually completing them before moving on to the next chapter. Seriously, don't just do them in your head. By getting your answers down on paper, you make them real and commit to your growth.

There are several basic areas you'll be coached on throughout this book in your quest for authentic success. Here's a preview of what to expect:

1. **Clarity:** Get crystal clear on what success means to you by defining a clear "desired outcome" and long-term goals for yourself.

   - First, we'll identify your core values—the root beliefs that form your foundation and guide you in your everyday life, personally and professionally.
   - We will dive into lifestyle priorities. What do you want your life to look like and feel like on a daily basis? Is creating and maintaining healthy relationships a priority? Or do you prefer to spend time in solitude, learning and reflecting?
   - Visualize your desires through long-term and short-term goal-setting and visioning exercises. We'll break your big aspirations down into bite-sized steps that are concrete and achievable.

2. **Mindset:** Overcome negative thoughts, limiting beliefs, or the "mean girl" in your head. By priming your mind for success, you create a strong mental framework for achieving what you want.

   - Identifying your "junk thoughts" is crucial. We all have that self-doubting bitch critic in our head beating us up, telling us we're not good enough. I'll coach you on how to become aware of the junk thoughts in your mind and take away their power.
   - You'll learn to reframe and flip those negative thoughts into truer, more empowering statements. Those doubts that creep into your mind aren't valid—they're total junk! We'll go through a proven process for turning negativity into empowerment.

- With a more empowered mindset, you'll select your Power Statements—the mantras that will guide you in your day-to-day life, giving you unshakeable confidence and setting you up for success.

3. **Your Authentic Style:** Every person is unique. Dive into identifying your personality, communication style, and behavioral tendencies so you can become more aware of who you are, how you behave, and how others perceive you. Having this deeper sense of self-awareness uncovers why you operate the way you do, enabling you to be intentional, strategic, and authentically YOU.

4. **Actions:** Pinpoint which specific actions, habits, and routines will enable you to achieve authentic success and get what you really want, both personally and professionally. Take concrete steps to start turning your goals into reality.

   - The quality of your habits determines the quality of your life. We'll ensure that you adopt and maintain habits that set you up for authentic success.
   - Creating intentional morning and nighttime routines can optimize and upgrade your life. There isn't just one right way to start or end your day, but there are many wrong ways. Craft routines that work for you! They can be highly customized in accordance with your available time, energy, and commitment level. We'll discuss how to be proactive about creating a day that increases your energy, expands your awareness, and allows more room for success and fulfillment in your life.

5. **Expansion:** Optimize your life to make your authentic success more efficient and effective.

   - Think about the last time you got a new job, seized a business opportunity, or made a new friend. I'll bet it was due to an introduction or referral from someone you know. Most great opportunities in your life are due to relationships. In fact, 85 percent of all jobs are landed through *networking*! The reality is that the people you spend the most time with make a dramatic impact on your life. Yet most women I know aren't leveraging their personal or professional networks effectively. Many of them perceive "networking" as a dirty word; they think it comes with being salesy or fake. We'll discuss how to build your network in a way that is aligned with your values, goals, and priorities. Having a warm, robust, and authentic network is a key way to expand your success.

- Having a fantastic mentor can be a game-changer. Great mentors will listen to you and guide you on your journey. They will support you and be a resource for you, without telling you what to do. They can enrich your life through education, guidance, and opening up new opportunities for you through *their* network. You should be willing to not just be a mentee but also to be a mentor for someone else on their journey. We'll discuss how the power of mentorship can expand your success.

6. **Outside Factors:** Learn how to be authentic when the world around you isn't making it easy to be authentically you. There are external factors that impact you, and navigating them is part of the journey.

- The rise of AI is sabotaging humans' ability to be authentic. Using AI to think or speak for you is stealing what makes you uniquely YOU. Using AI as a tool to make you more productive, polished, and efficient is great. But be careful that it's not diluting who you are and taking away the human element that makes you authentic. We'll discuss how to stay authentically human in our AI-driven world.

- Life can be shitty. How do you maintain your authenticity and resilience even when life is tough? Inevitably, there will be challenges. You'll have a health crisis at the worst possible time, your car will break down, your company will announce layoffs—we all face endless challenges. What's important is how you navigate those challenges. Building perseverance, resilience, and grit is key to conquering the obstacles you face along the way.

Your journey to authentic success begins now!

But first, let's meet! Scan the QR code below to watch a personal welcome video from me. I'm so excited you're here and I can't wait to be part of your journey.

Clarity: Discover What Authentic Success Means to You

When I was a little kid, my family would drive around my hometown of Houston every December to look at the holiday lights. We would always go to the most affluent neighborhood in the city, where the best and most elaborate decorations could be found. Each scene was carefully arranged by a team of hired landscapers. We would comment on how nice it would be to live in a "million-dollar home." I had no idea how much those homes actually cost (although the prices have probably increased like crazy since the '90s), but my parents routinely used the phrase "million-dollar home," so I did, too.

Watching the brightly colored Santas and elves and the light-up icicles draped over massive oak trees, I thought to myself, "I want to live in a million-dollar home someday. That's how I'll know *I've made it.*"

To my 8-year-old self, living in a million-dollar home was the definition of success.

As I write this in 2025, I'm living in San Diego, California, where, according to Zillow data, the **average** home costs $1 million. I see million-dollar homes every day, and some of them are dumps! Comparing Houston home prices from the '90s and Southern California home prices in 2025 is comparing apples to oranges. But my point is that *my definition of success has changed.* I no longer view living in a million-dollar home as the gold standard of success. There are many other ways I would measure my success that have nothing at all to do with a million-dollar home or the price of my home.

What you consider "success" changes as you change. It's natural. There is no success box that you can put yourself in. If there were, you'd probably want to find your way out of that box in just a few years' time!

In the same way your perception of success changes throughout your life, success also differs from person to person.

When I was a brand-new business owner posting on Instagram, I thought getting 15 likes on a post was a massive success! However, to someone like Jay Shetty, who has a massive following, 15 likes on an Instagram post would probably feel like a huge flop—the opposite of success. Those 15 likes meant something different for me than they did for him. For me, they were progress. For him, they would be a problem. Our individual perspectives, desires, and goals affect how we perceive success.

A 2019 Gallup poll found that Americans' views of success change based on a variety of factors, such as gender, household income, and ideological differences. It makes sense that different demographic groups view it differently.

But does it matter what success means to every other American? In this book, I'm more concerned about what success means to YOU.

Do you know what success means to you? When was the last time you really articulated it by writing it down or saying it out loud? "This is what success means to me, world!"

A few of you reading this will say, "Sure, I know exactly what success means to me. I can exactly describe the detailed life I want that would mean I'm authentically successful." If that's you, please proceed straight to Chapter 2. Otherwise, keep reading.

You can't determine what success means to you without determining your core values.

To achieve *authentic* success, it needs to be based on the things you value most. Your core values are the root beliefs that you operate from, the principles that guide you in your everyday life, personally and professionally. While your core values can evolve over time, they tend to be more fixed than other factors.

Your core values are the beliefs that you stand behind and live your life by. They dictate your thoughts, feelings, and actions, even if you're unaware that they do. They drive your success at work, the way you show up in relationships, and even how you manage your money. They are at the **core** of everything you do.

Many people sleepwalk through life, unaware of their core values. They aren't *intentionally* acting from their values, which leads to misalignment, a lack of fulfillment, and success that eludes them. Maybe you're someone who values reliability. You pride yourself on being a spouse, friend, and coworker who can be counted on, and you appreciate the same in others. Let's say you're going through a tough time and have a lot on your plate. Your stress is through the roof, you're not sleeping well, and you desperately want to get out of your current work situation. Because of everything on your plate, the overwhelm takes over. You show up late to a work meeting because you're distracted. You cancel dinner plans with your friend at the last minute because you're exhausted and just want to go home.

Stress makes you act in ways that aren't consistent with the reliable person you strive to be. You value reliability, yet you realize that people can't really depend on you right now. Your actions and values are misaligned. This leads to further stress, an ache in your gut, and a feeling of failure.

When you know your core values and leverage them intentionally, you can achieve success in an authentic way.

Let's now identify your core values. I put core values into two different categories: *relationships* and *results*. The things you value are often directly related to either your relationships with other people or the results you're creating in your life.

Core Values Bracket Exercise

First, look below at the two lists of words under **Relationships** and **Results.** Select the eight core values from each list that resonate with you the most and write each word on a line of your bracket on the corresponding side. Relationship words go down the left side; results words go down the right side. The words you choose should be the words you feel most strongly about at this time in your life. If there's a word or phrase that comes to mind that isn't on either list, you can write it in as one of your top values.

Just like a March Madness tournament bracket, you're going to have your core values on each side compete against each other. Write the "winning" core value from each matchup on the next (interior) line, getting closer to the center.

Continue to fill out all the lines on your Core Values Bracket in the same fashion until it is clear who the top two winners are, one relationships value and one results value.

Don't just complete this exercise in your head—complete it with pen and paper. If you can't write in this book or you're listening to an audiobook, grab a scratch sheet of paper and create an ad hoc bracket for yourself.

RELATIONSHIPS	**RESULTS**
Respect, Selflessness, Accountability, Collaboration, Community, Recognition, Equality, Forgiveness, Courtesy, Care, Consistency, Honesty, Flexibility, Appreciation, Belonging, Initiative, Calmness, Empathy, Encouragement, Loyalty, Patience, Play, Reliability, Spirituality, Self-Control, Sophistication, Thoughtfulness, Humor, Trust, Unity, Popularity, Positivity, Communication, Coachability, Assertiveness	Discipline, Passion, Change, Vision, Bravery, Knowledge, Advancement, Adaptability, Tenacity, Imagination, Resilience, Responsibility, Creativity, Courage, Achievement, Commitment, Enthusiasm, Boldness, Competence, Energy, Ethics, Excellence, Fun, Individuality, Learning, Making A Difference, Optimism, Preparation, Resourcefulness, Wisdom, Sacrifice, Focus, Ownership

Select your top 8
RELATIONSHIPS values and
write them on this side.

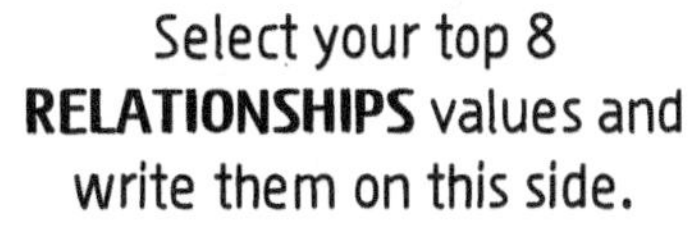

Select your top 8
RESULTS values and write
them on this side.

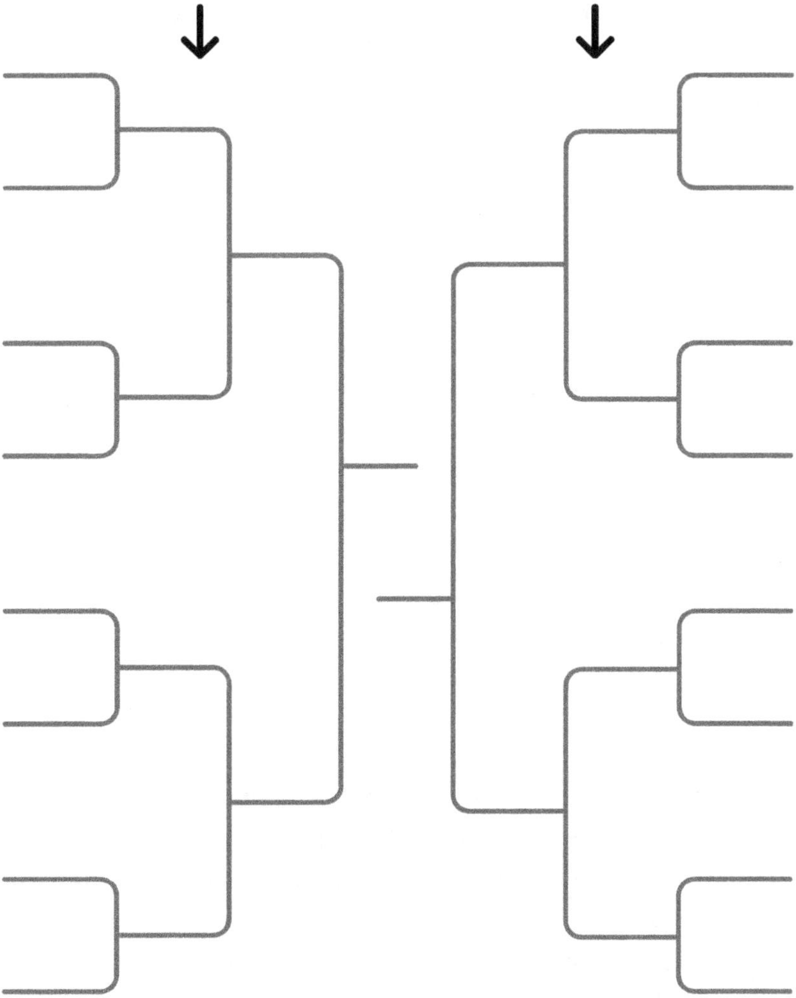

Let's now take a deeper look at the core values you selected.

Relationships Value:

What is your top core value related to relationships? This value sets the stage for every relationship in your life. Now, self-reflect and write your answers to the questions below:

Question:	Your Answer:
How does the core value I chose show up in my relationships?	
Do I display this value through my <u>words</u> to other people on a daily basis?	
Do I display this through my <u>actions</u> toward other people on a daily basis?	
What would it look like for me to truly embody ____________ (your relationship value) in my day-to-day life as I interact with others?	
How would I know and how would others know that this is my core value?	

When it comes to relationships, it's difficult to be everything to everybody. This is especially challenging if you're a people pleaser. You want to make everybody else happy all the time. We'll address people-pleasing more in a later chapter, but for now let's consider how acting from your core values might improve your relationships rather than constantly being a "yes-ma'am" or a "yes-man."

By embodying your relationship core value each day, you develop your personal and professional relationships around the value that matters the most to you. Most people don't live their lives like this. They aren't thinking about their values and how to live them on a daily basis.

My coaching client, Melanie, landed a new job. After working for 15 years in sales as a manager, she was hired by a new company as a director. Melanie was thrilled about her promotion and the increase in responsibility. She was also nervous about how she would build strong relationships with her new team and set herself up for success as a leader at the company. She wanted to do ALL the things she thought great leaders should do, but it seemed overwhelming to "do it all."

Melanie completed her Core Values Bracket and chose **communication** as her top relationship value. She realized that communication was what made or broke all of her relationships in the past. A big reason she wanted to leave her company and work elsewhere was that she didn't feel as though the company had effective communication from the top down. She was excited about her new company because the leadership team and her new boss gave her reason to believe that the communication would be more transparent and effective, aligning with Melanie's core value of communication.

This realization inspired Melanie to step into her new role as a leader with strong communication skills. She knew strong communication would be the means of building rapport with her new team and establishing herself as a leader to people at all levels. She committed to being a role model of excellent communication to her new team.

Then, we took it one step further, and Melanie identified concrete actions she could take at work to embody her core value of communication. Here were a few actions she decided on:

- Weekly one-on-one check-ins with direct reports
- Asking team members their preferred method of receiving feedback
- A focus on being concise during meetings
- Clear expectations and boundaries around appropriate communication
- Weekly office hours for drop-in questions and discussion

Acting with your core values in mind will help you be more authentic, genuine, and effective in any role, but especially as a leader. When your actions are in alignment with your values, not only will you have stronger relationships, but those relationships will also be more authentic.

Results Value:

What is your top core value related to results? This value is what determines the outcomes you see in every area of life. Self-reflect and write your answers to the questions below:

Question:	Your Answer:
How does the core value I chose impact the results I see in my life?	
Do I display this value in my <u>work</u> on a daily basis?	
Do I display this value in my <u>personal life</u> on a daily basis?	
What would it look like for me to truly embody ____________ (your results core value) in my day-to-day life?	
From what is happening in my life, what evidence would suggest that this is my core value?	

Results are the concrete outcomes or impacts of the actions you take. Your values, words, and actions all play a big part in getting results.

It sounds simple, right?

Work harder, make more money.

Eat less junk food, lose 10 pounds.

But, as anyone who has failed to reach a goal before knows, achieving success is more complex than this. It's not a straight line from point A to point B.

Your results core value sets the stage for the outcomes in your life. When you intentionally live your core value, it will dictate your actions and behaviors, which will dictate your words and your habits, which will ultimately dictate your results.

With the awareness of your results core value, you can take action to achieve the success you desire.

My client, Danielle, was a new business owner. She was two years into running her dental practice in Boston. While she had made some good progress in her business's nascent years, she was finding it difficult to generate consistent leads, which ultimately meant that her income was spiking up and down from month to month and her stress was through the roof.

Danielle selected **commitment** as her top results core value. Before starting her business, in her years studying to become a dentist, her commitment to her studies during dental school is what landed her at the top of her DDS program. Commitment to great parenting is what made her a fantastic mother to her two young children.

But Danielle realized she wasn't showing commitment when it came to her dental business.

She was showing up haphazardly each day, taking inconsistent action. Every business owner has heard the saying "throwing spaghetti at the wall to see what sticks," and that's exactly what Danielle was doing. Through an honest coaching conversation, Danielle admitted that although she appeared to be committed to her business, she had one foot in and one foot out, afraid to fully commit and go "all in" on being a successful self-employed dentist.

I asked Danielle, "As someone who values commitment, what would it look like to embody commitment in your business on a daily basis?" She knew it would take consistency in her marketing efforts, networking on a regular basis, and putting her sign outside her office each day (her office was on a heavily trafficked street in Boston). These were all simple actions, but her lack of commitment was preventing her from doing them while also making her feel awful about herself because she was blatantly disregarding her core values.

Next, I asked her, "What results might you experience in your business if you embodied your value of commitment to your business on a daily basis?" This is when Danielle told me that she KNEW in her heart of hearts that if she really committed, she would experience:

- Consistent referrals from her networking partners
- Leads pouring in through her email inbox and foot traffic daily
- A jam-packed schedule full of dental patients
- A much higher income that didn't rise and fall each month, but was more predictable and more stable

Danielle knew it was a no-brainer. It was time to fully embrace her core value of commitment and apply it to her business.

With her new awareness, Danielle committed and got to work. She began networking more regularly, put her sign outside daily, and pushed back against "shiny object syndrome." She started having more consistent leads pour in and achieved her highest revenue months ever, which consistently grew month after month.

Like Danielle, you should consider how your core values drive your actions, which drive your results. Now that you have awareness of your core values, how can you be proactive and strategic about living them on a daily basis to create success in your life? Can you pinpoint the specific steps you would need to take to make this happen? If so, write them down and commit to them!

Your core values are the root beliefs that you operate from, guiding you in your everyday life. Keep your core values at the forefront of your mind and tap into them regularly to create the relationships and results that will lead to authentic success.

Building a Lifestyle of Authentic Success

Authentic success hinges on the lifestyle you create. What do you want your life to look and feel like on a daily basis? There's a lot that plays into your "lifestyle," but ultimately, a lifestyle that satisfies your priorities and leads to positive emotions is what defines authentic success.

We're going to focus on these seven main areas of life:

1. Health
2. Career
3. Home Environment
4. Finances
5. Relationships
6. That Which Is Greater
7. Hobbies and Interests

Remember that "million-dollar home" that defined success for me as a child? That was a "finances" and "home environment" lifestyle priority for me. Oftentimes, you'll find that what you view as success is about the lifestyle you enjoy and how that lifestyle makes you **feel**.

When you achieve success and create the lifestyle you want, many positive emotions come with that. It could be happiness, pride, excitement, joy, or gratitude. Authentic success is feeling those emotions as a result of the lifestyle you've created, while staying true to yourself and aligned with your values.

Dream-Big Lifestyle Exercise

What does an authentically successful lifestyle look like to you? This exercise is to help you get clear on that dream lifestyle. For each of the seven areas below, brainstorm what it would mean to be authentically successful in that area. Allow yourself to **dream big** during this exercise and imagine all the possibilities available to you.

Complete the chart below by writing three to five bullet points or sentences that capture what that Dream-Big Lifestyle area would be for you at your most successful. There's a filled-out chart on the following page to show you an example of the completed exercise.

Health Your physical, mental, and emotional well-being	
Career Your full-time work or professional life	
Home Environment Your home, living space, neighborhood, community, and overall environment	
Finances Your money – salary, savings, investments, debt, and money mindset	

Relationships Your friends, family, significant other, as well as professional relationships	
Hobbies and Interests The things you enjoy doing in your personal time	
That Which Is Greater Your faith, religion, spirituality, or connection to your sense of purpose	

Here's an example of a filled-out version of the chart:

Health Your physical, mental, and emotional well-being	Sleeping peacefully 8 hours nightly Maintaining a healthy weight and feeling confident in my body Feeling little stress and able to handle stress in healthy ways Exercising 3-4 times weekly Eating healthy, nourishing foods that energize my body

Career Your full-time work or professional life	Working for a company that is doing something good for the world Holding a senior director-level role, leading a team Having a remote job with flexible working hours Making $250,000+ Feeling respected, appreciated, and valued by my organization
Home Environment Your home, living space, neighborhood, community, and overall environment	Living in a large home with a front yard and backyard Having neighbors I am friends/friendly with and enjoy seeing Hosting friends at my house regularly, holding backyard BBQs Working at a home office I love that is conducive to successful work Living within walking distance to the ocean (10-15 minutes)
Finances Your money – salary, savings, investments, debt, and money mindset	Being debt-free! Contributing to a retirement fund Taking quarterly vacations without worrying about prices Setting plenty aside to pay for kids' college Having enough to buy a lake house in addition to a primary home
Relationships Your friends, family, significant other, as well as professional relationships	Planning weekly date nights with my husband Having regular calls and texts with my closest girlfriends and traveling together once annually Feeling deeply connected within my women's professional networking group, with in-person events at least once a month Holding Sunday dinners with the family—love and connection

That Which Is Greater Your faith, religion, spirituality, or connection to your sense of purpose	Feeling like my job is purposeful and serves a greater good Keeping a daily reflection practice before work each morning Feeling a strong sense of contribution and positive impact Feeling a connection to a higher power
Hobbies and Interests The things you enjoy doing in your personal time	Reading novels I enjoy every night before bed Continuing to paint and hone my creative skills Taking quarterly vacations to places where I can hike in nature Running two half-marathons annually Spending time with friends, cooking meals for them, and hosting dinner parties

Your Dream-Big Lifestyle exercise will help you gain clarity on what you want your life to look and feel like. Some things you wrote may already be part of your lifestyle now, while others might seem like an impossible dream. Either way is OK. This isn't about judging your current lifestyle; it's about determining what authentic success would actually look like for you. It's about being aware of the things that would bring positivity and joy into your life.

With this clarity around your lifestyle priorities, you can start breaking down your journey to authentic success into goals and milestones, which we'll be doing in later chapters.

Visualize Authentic Success

"Watch your thoughts, they become your words; watch your words, they become your actions; watch your actions, they become your habits; watch your habits, they become your character; watch your character, it becomes your destiny." – Lao Tzu, ancient Chinese philosopher

You might already be familiar with the power that your thoughts hold. Everything you want to achieve in this life starts in your mind.

Authentic success starts in your mind. If your thoughts are negative or disempowering, chances are that your words, actions, and results are also negative or disempowering. On the flip side, when your thoughts are positive and empowering, they fuel success and will create positive results in your life.

Visualization is creating mental images in your mind with the purpose of achieving a specific goal or result. It's a creative process that involves being imaginative, curious, and focused on a desired outcome.

You've probably heard of celebrities who credit their success to visualization. Steve Jobs used visualization to help him envision the future of Apple and prepare for product launches. In 1995, Jim Carrey wrote himself a fictional check for $10 million for "acting services rendered" to motivate himself, and three years later landed the role in "Dumb and Dumber" for $10 million. In 2015, Carli Lloyd visualized herself scoring four goals before a soccer game and went on to score three, becoming the first woman in World Cup history to do so.

Many athletes, entrepreneurs, actors, and other successful individuals have publicly talked about their "mental rehearsals." Envisioning the outcome they want to achieve prepares them for real-life success.

What Does Visualization Have to Do with Authentic Success?

Visualizing your authentic success will help you achieve it that much faster. It will help you stay more focused, motivated, prepared, confident, and excited. It will also improve your performance on a consistent basis. You can even visualize yourself overcoming potential challenges or obstacles you might encounter ('cause there *will* be challenges!), which makes them that much easier to tackle when they happen in real life.

Having completed your Core Values Bracket and Dream-Big Lifestyle exercises, you now have clarity on what authentic success looks like to you in terms of your values and lifestyles. Let's use this clarity as a starting point to visualize your success.

The best way to visualize is the way that you can practice consistently. Whatever tool you choose for visualizing, make sure it's something you can keep up with daily. Here are some strategies I've had my coaching clients try:

- **Journaling:** Write down your ideal outcome of authentic success. This could be a "dream day" told in narrative format. Write down exactly what happened throughout the day, from the time you woke up, what you ate, who you interacted with, what you did at work, and everything in between. Make sure to include your emotions and how good it felt to be living this life.

- **Mental rehearsal:** Close your eyes and form a mental image in your brain of yourself achieving ideal success. Try to slip yourself right into the body of that version of you that already has the authentic success you desire. Form a clear picture in your mind's eye of yourself going through the day, using your senses to bring details to life.

- **Vision boards:** Create a vision board, which includes pictures, quotes, words, or other visuals that are representations of authentic success—the future you are creating. Hang your vision board somewhere you'll see it regularly, like in front of your desk at work, or set it as the background on your computer monitor.

- **Guided meditations:** There are so many apps, videos, platforms, and YouTube channels out there with guided meditations you can use. Simply Google "guided meditation for achieving success," and you'll find thousands of options.

- **Affirmations:** These are positive statements you say aloud to yourself. Our lives are shaped by the words we speak. By saying affirmations out loud daily, you create positive self-talk that helps cultivate a positive mindset of authentic success.

Use all your senses when you visualize. Get hyper-focused on your authentic success and how it looks, feels, sounds, smells, and tastes. If you're doing a mental rehearsal, create the clearest, most vivid picture you can. Imagine the sounds in this future reality of yours. Are people talking? What are they saying to you? Notice what's around you and observe the tiny details, like the smell of the perfume you're wearing or the taste of the red wine you're drinking. The little details matter—they add richness and detail to your vision.

Take 10 minutes every day for visualization. The best time to visualize is either in the morning or evening, when you're first waking up or about to go to sleep. This helps engage your subconscious mind to focus on what you want.

While visualization isn't a novel concept, it can be challenging to integrate into your life consistently if you're not used to doing it regularly. Like any other new habit, it takes time to make it a routine. Set a 10-minute timer every day, at the same time each day, and dedicate that time to visualization. Commit to trying it for 30 days and embed it into your life as a daily habit. Not only will this keep you motivated and focused, it will also accelerate your results.

Chapter 1 Recap:

1. Complete the Core Values Bracket Exercise and select your top core values for relationships and results. Answer the self-reflection questions for each value.

2. For each of your top two core values, create a list of four to six concrete actions you can take that are representative of those values. Put those actions into practice on a daily basis!

3. Complete the Dream-Big Lifestyle Exercise to get clarity on what you *really* want your life to look and feel like.

4. Use visualization techniques to stay focused, motivated, prepared, confident, and excited about your vision of success. Visualization prepares you for real-life success and accelerates your results.

All of the exercises and reflection questions in this book can be accessed digitally. I've created downloadable versions of everything, including the Core Values Bracket and Dream Big Lifestyle worksheets from Chapter 1. Scan the QR code below to access them all for free.

The Mindset Makeover: Your Path to Authentic Confidence

"Whether you think you can, or you think you can't, you're right." – Henry Ford, American industrialist and founder of Ford Motor Company

Unless you've been living under a rock for the last 20 years, chances are that you've read or heard about "mindset"—a hugely popular topic in the world of self-development. In short, mindset means that what you believe about yourself impacts your success or your failure, that your thoughts become your reality.

Carol Dweck's 2007 book *Mindset: The New Psychology of Success* was the impetus for many people to consciously begin thinking about how their mindset impacts their success. Dweck, a renowned Stanford University psychologist, shows how success in school, work, sports, the arts, and almost every area of your life is dramatically impacted by how you think about yourself—your talents, abilities, and skills.

Your mindset consists of everything going on in your brain, conscious and unconscious. This includes things like your confidence, self-belief, determination to succeed, and ability to overcome rejection. Your mindset is so important because your thoughts and emotions are the catalyst for the results you create in your life. If you've ever struggled with procrastination, lack of consistency, self-doubt, fear of failure, or feeling stuck in life, this all stems from your mindset.

You will only be as successful, joyful, and energetic as your mindset allows you to be.

Cultivating a mindset of authentic success is crucial to being authentically successful. In order to do this, your thoughts need to be rooted in self-belief, confidence, and empowerment. The problem with this is that so many people hold many negative thoughts about themselves, others, and the state of the world.

In 2020, psychology experts at Queen's University in Canada conducted a study that determined the average person has approximately 6,000 thoughts every day. Of those thoughts, 80 percent are *negative*! Do the math, and it's easy to see why so many people aren't achieving authentic success.... Our brains are constantly being barraged by self-limiting negativity! Do any of these thoughts below sound familiar to you?

- "Ugh, I slept terribly. Today is going to be a rough day."
- "There's no way I can get all of this done. I don't have enough time."
- "I wish my partner would contribute more. I'm doing all the work here."
- "Fuck this traffic, I'm going to be late AGAIN!"
- "I'm having a bad hair day."
- "Do my kids think I'm their chauffeur or something?"
- "I look fat in this dress."
- "No one ever notices when I do good things. I just want to be appreciated."
- "If I raise my prices, I'll lose clients."
- "If I speak my mind, people aren't going to take me seriously."

These are just examples of the negative thoughts that might be playing on a loop in your mind throughout the day. I've seen it with my clients, and I've seen it with myself. Without even noticing it, we think negatively almost all day long. And it's hard to be successful when we're hyperfocused on the bad, even if it's by accident.

There's good news, though. By bringing awareness and intentionality to your thoughts, you can learn to actively choose the more positive thoughts, priming your mind for success. Think about it like going to the gym, but instead of working out your muscles, you're working out your mind.

This chapter focuses on how you can bring awareness to your thoughts so you can use your mind to build more confidence and self-belief, ultimately enabling you to achieve the success you desire. Ready for your mindset makeover?

Understanding Your Negative Thoughts

To develop a positive mindset, you first need to understand your negative thoughts. What are they, and where do they come from?

Many of your negative thoughts likely stem from experiences you've had throughout your lifetime, going all the way back to when you were a child. In fact, the experiences you had in your formative years probably contribute more to your negative thoughts than any other life experiences. Your childhood is when you were most impressionable and developed your thoughts, beliefs, and attitudes about yourself and about life.

One of my coaching clients, Mary, was a first-generation Japanese immigrant. She described her childhood as full of intense pressure, especially when it came to her education. Her parents not only pushed her to succeed academically but also put a strong emphasis on being THE best. Being in the top 5 percent of her high school class "wasn't good enough"—she needed to be in the top 1 percent of her class. It was drilled into her as a teenager that she had to academically outperform her peers—all of them—to meet her parents' standards and expectations. That was tough for Mary. She graduated near the top of her class and attended a prestigious university but never quite felt "good enough." She wasn't the valedictorian, she wasn't the class president, and she was constantly being pushed by her parents to be even better.

In her 20s, Mary went to graduate school and became a Doctor of Chiropractic. She started her own business and was highly skilled at her practice, helping her patients (many of whom were accomplished athletes) to overcome chronic pain. Despite the great results her patients got from working with her, Mary struggled to attract new patients and thrive in her business. In our coaching, it became obvious that Mary had huge mindset blocks that were preventing her from achieving authentic success in her chiropractic business.

As an adult woman in her 30s, Mary felt like she was never good enough. She told me that she wanted to be a "top 1 percent chiropractor," but didn't believe she could ever get there. She put intense pressure on herself to be THE best, much as her parents did when she was in high school. While there's nothing wrong with striving to be great, Mary's unhealthy obsession with being the best was causing her to crumble mentally and emotionally. Feeling like she could never measure up to her own high expectations made her constantly feel like she was failing. And it wasn't helping her get any closer to being authentically successful.

Throughout her coaching, Mary and I talked at length about her relationship with her parents and the huge amount of pressure they constantly put on her. Mary came to understand that the pressure from her parents served her well as a teenager with high educational ambitions. They drove her to succeed academically, to get into a great university, and to ultimately graduate from chiropractic school with honors. She appreciated that she was able to achieve these milestones with her parents' encouragement.

However, Mary also began to understand that those childhood experiences were responsible for her negative beliefs about herself, her business, and what she was capable of. She flat-out told me, "I don't feel good enough at what I do. It doesn't feel like enough. I want to be in the top 1 percent of all chiropractors." Identifying her negative thoughts and being able to trace them back to childhood was a huge part of Mary taking ownership of her mindset.

Self-awareness is key when it comes to mastering your mindset. Mary understood her negative thoughts clearly. She also understood where the thoughts came from (her parents) and how it was impacting her ability to be successful in her business.

Your parents and childhood aren't the only sources of negative thoughts. They may also stem from:

- Societal pressures and expectations
- Comparison to others, especially on social media
- Fear of failure or success
- Imposter syndrome
- Low self-esteem
- Criticism from others
- Unrealistic standards you see in the media
- Cultural or family beliefs
- Stress and burnout
- Physical health issues or chronic pain
- Gender or racial stereotypes or biases
- Work-related pressures

And more! This list isn't all-encompassing. Additionally, these sources often overlap and interact, creating complex patterns of negative thinking.

By understanding your negative thoughts and identifying where they come from, you can bring awareness to your mindset, which is always the first step to making a change. Awareness precedes action, and action precedes success.

What Are YOUR Negative Thoughts?

Now that you understand negative thoughts and how they impact your life, let's identify YOUR negative thoughts. We all have them! Start with a list of the five or 10 negative thoughts that creep into your mind and give you a sense of self-doubt, limitation, or the feeling that, "I can't do this because...." These aren't just those pesky, annoying thoughts that arrive one minute and leave the next. These are the ones that return time and time again, often bringing self-doubt with them.

Here are some of the most common negative thoughts I hear from my clients:

- "I'm too young."
- "I'm too old."
- "I don't have the right experience."
- "I'm not attractive enough."
- "I'm not smart enough."
- "I'm not a leader; I'm a follower."
- "I'm a failure. I've done so many things wrong, and I'll probably keep failing."
- "Everyone around me is better than I am."
- "I'm 'behind' in life."
- "Nobody takes me seriously."
- "I won't be successful. I'll never make it."
- "I'm not likable. People don't naturally like me."
- "Anything that can go wrong will go wrong."
- "I could never make THAT much money."

Now that you have some examples, write down your own negative thoughts. What are the five or 10 negative thoughts that creep into your mind, hitting your confidence or beating you down? Don't just think of them in your head; take the time to write them down in the box below.

<table>
<tr><td>My Negative Thoughts:</td></tr>
<tr><td>

</td></tr>
</table>

According to psychologists who specialize in Cognitive Behavioral Therapy (CBT), thought journaling is another effective exercise to help you identify your negative thoughts throughout the day. Keep a "thought journal" nearby throughout the day and start writing down thoughts as they come up, especially the negative ones. This can help you become aware of recurring patterns.

Clearly identifying your negative thoughts is an important part of taking away their power. Just by noticing them and saying, "Hey, I recognize you and notice that you're there," you're taking one small step toward no longer letting these thoughts subconsciously sabotage your mind without your permission.

Some of my coaching clients like to give their negative thoughts a name. They'll name their negative thoughts something like Cruella, Regina George, or even "that bitch in my head."

I like this strategy for two reasons. First, it implies that these thoughts aren't yours. It recognizes that there's a bit of self-sabotage going on inside your mind and that you're simply observing it. Second, it gives your negative thoughts a name so you can easily identify and bring self-awareness to them in a way that almost feels like you're catching yourself in the act. I have had a client say, "Cruella's voice was reeeeally loud this week. I had to tell her to shut up!"

It's also important to recognize the role of triggers in activating these negative thoughts. Sometimes, these negative thoughts may just appear out of thin air because that's what they've been doing for years. But other times, these negative thoughts will come up when something happens in your life to trigger them.

Triggers might include:

- A tough conversation with a friend or colleague
- Rejection
- Financial stress
- Comparing yourself to someone else
- Making mistakes or "failing"
- Health issues or physical pain
- Being in unfamiliar or uncomfortable situations
- Seeing others succeed where you've struggled
- Stressful deadlines or important events
- Reminders of past traumas or experiences

Triggers can be highly individual, and I encourage you to reflect on your own personal triggers. If you're struggling at work and feel like you aren't respected or appreciated by your boss, it might be a trigger when you talk to your best friend and hear that she is thriving at work, just got a promotion and salary increase, and is gushing about how happy and fulfilled she feels at work. This might trigger a flurry of negative thoughts in your own head:

- *I won't ever be as successful as she is.*
- *No one takes me seriously.*
- *I'm a failure.*

Start to notice your personal triggers and be aware of the negative thoughts that come up when facing them.

The Power of Reframing

Now that you have your list of five or 10 negative thoughts, let's talk about what to do with them. You probably wish you could say, "I don't want to think that thought anymore. Goodbye!" We would all do that if we could and get rid of our negative thoughts immediately. In reality, most of your negative thoughts are repetitive. You've been ruminating on them for days, weeks, months, years, and maybe decades. To tell yourself, "I simply don't think that way anymore," wouldn't be honest or authentic.

Instead, I coach my clients on **reframing** their negative thoughts. While it's hard to completely flip your mindset right away, it's almost always possible to consider thoughts that are *more positive* or *truer* than the negative BS you have been repeating in your head.

Go through your list of negative thoughts one by one. For each negative thought, complete the following sentences:

- A more positive way of seeing this is....
- That's not totally true because....
- A more powerful way to reframe this thought would be....

Take your time to do this for every thought on your list. Sit down and write them out. The most important one is the third bullet: "A more powerful way to reframe this thought would be…." Whatever your reframe statement is, it should be something that resonates with you and feels authentic. We're not looking for some magic wand that doesn't feel realistic or genuine. It should be a reframe that feels reasonable and reachable.

To recall Mary's experience, her negative thoughts were, "I don't feel good enough about what I do. It doesn't feel like enough. I want to be in the top 1 percent." Mary knew that ranking chiropractors was arbitrary and illogical, but these negative thoughts *aren't* logical. Her programming from childhood threw logic out the window and made her feel underaccomplished.

Here's how Mary completed the above sentences to reframe her negative thoughts:

- A more positive way of seeing this is… *This intense pressure helped me grow and succeed during hard times, but it no longer serves me anymore, and that's OK.*
- That's not totally true because… *I can be an amazing chiropractor without putting this intense pressure on myself to be in the top 1 percent.*
- A more powerful way to reframe this thought would be… *I choose to work from a place of joy and to serve my patients while also loving myself.*

After working through her reframe, Mary felt an immediate light bulb go off in her brain as she realized that she had the power to better understand her negative thoughts and shift her thinking. It was liberating to recognize that the pressure that once pushed her to succeed was no longer serving her. She realized that she didn't need to put that pressure on herself to be "the top 1 percent" anymore—it was stealing her joy. She chose to reframe her negative thoughts into something that felt much more empowering and positive: **I choose to work from a place of joy and to serve my patients while also loving myself.** This statement resonated with Mary and felt authentic.

Sometimes, the act of writing your first reframe will be your eureka moment, and your mindset will be altered forever. But if you're like many people, the process of reframing your negative thoughts is ongoing. You can't just do it once and expect that your mind will forever be changed. It requires continuous effort over several months. With most of my clients, I've found that after 30-60 days, the reframing becomes automatic and the negative thoughts get a lot quieter.

During your ongoing process of reframing, here's what it should look like, step by step:

1. Bring awareness to your negative thoughts and notice when they come up. *Be vigilant of your thoughts.*

2. When the negative thoughts come up, pause and call them out. "Oh, that's Cruella in my head again. The negative thoughts are there right now." Call them out <u>in the moment</u>.

3. Run your reframed thoughts right then and there. At first, this might require you to go back to your notes or open up your journal to revisit your reframing. Soon you'll have them memorized.

4. Say your reframed thoughts out loud to yourself three times—slowly and clearly. Try to really feel it in your body as you say it, taking a deep breath after each time you say it.

5. Move on with your day—that's it!

Since some of your negative thoughts have been part of your brain for decades, it may take time to reframe and unravel them. Stick with the process above consistently for 60 days, being hyperaware of your thoughts and focused on your reframing of them. You'll start to notice that you're in a much better headspace and your mind is primed for positivity and success. It will become easier to create the results you want to see in your life, and you will feel like your brain and body are in alignment.

Some days, the negative thoughts will be louder than others. This could be due to the triggers we discussed earlier, activating negative thoughts. Or you might be simply having a crappy day. That's OK.

Avoiding your negative thoughts or brushing them off won't get you where you want to be. On the days that your negative thoughts are louder, it's even *more important* to stick with the process of reframing and take the time to be aware of the negativity in your mind, even when it's uncomfortable.

Crafting Your Power Statements

Once you reframe your negative thoughts, you'll see that some of your reframes feel especially empowering and authentic. These are the reframes that resonate the MOST and really get you fired up and thinking differently. These are your **Power Statements.** I ask my coaching clients to determine their Power Statements by choosing the top three reframes that feel the most powerful and personal to them.

Here are Mary's Power Statements:

1. I choose to work from a place of joy and to serve my clients while also loving myself.
2. I am smart enough, good enough, and worthy of love.
3. My services are of the highest quality, and people are willing to pay a premium price for the immense value that I provide.

Now it's your turn. Go back to your list of reframes and choose the top three statements that feel the most positive and empowering to you. Make sure that every word feels authentic and believable. A Power Statement that you don't really resonate with or that doesn't feel true or empowering isn't going to serve you. Write them down in the box below:

My Power Statements
1.
2.
3.

Once, I was working with a client who was looking for a new job. She had more than 10 job interviews in a nine-month period, but zero offers. A few of her negative thoughts were, "I suck at job interviews. I don't know how to stand out from other applicants. I'll never get hired." Initially, she reframed this into, "I am fantastic at job interviews and know how to ace them and get the job." Upon closer inspection, she realized that reframe didn't feel quite true or authentic—it didn't really resonate with her. We worked together to tweak the reframe into something that felt more genuine: "I am generally well-liked and do OK during interviews. I'm in the process of improving my interview skills so I can get that extra 'oomph' and finally land a job. With just a little more practice, it will happen!"

If you need to revise any of your reframes so they feel the truest and most empowering for you, go for it.

Once you've identified your top three Power Statements, it's important to integrate them into daily life. Write them down and put them somewhere you'll see regularly. You could put them on a sticky note on your bathroom mirror, display them on a bulletin board in front of your desk, or keep them in the Notes app of your phone. The point is to put them somewhere you can see them often and refer back to them throughout the day.

Beyond writing them down, saying your Power Statements out loud daily makes them more impactful. Find five minutes daily to say them aloud to yourself. This can be in the bathroom mirror as you're getting ready for the day, in your office chair as you're prepping for the workday ahead, or even as you're taking the dog on a morning walk. At first, you might be reading them, but eventually they should be memorized. It's also important to say them out loud *with conviction*. Say it like you mean it! Make a point to slow down and focus on the words you're saying and align yourself with them. This enhances the effectiveness of your Power Statements.

Go back to your Power Statements throughout the day. Maybe you need a boost of encouragement, a quick reminder of your power, or to recenter your mind. Your Power Statements are a tool for you to access the power and positivity in your brain. Use them as needed in your daily life.

The Impact of Your Mindset Makeover

As your mindset improves, other aspects of your life will improve, too. This book is about success, and you'll certainly be more successful if your thoughts are more positive and empowering rather than negative and full of doubt. Your thoughts are the catalyst for the results you create in your life.

Yes, a strong mindset will improve your professional life. You'll overcome challenges more quickly and efficiently, you'll be solutions-oriented rather than problem-focused, you'll open yourself up to more job or business opportunities, and you'll likely make more money.

Your mindset makeover doesn't just apply to your professional life; it extends to other areas of your life as well. A positive mindset will improve your relationships with yourself and others. You'll show up as a better partner, friend, parent, or sibling. You'll communicate better, you won't blame others for your problems, and people will find you more enjoyable to be around. You'll find your relationships become more fulfilling. Generally speaking, you'll be more content in your personal relationships.

Mary's improved mindset was the first step to growing her business. With a new belief in herself, she got out of her own way, and her chiropractic practice started to grow. She was seeing more and more patients each week, increasing her revenue, and expanding her positive impact on patients' health. But it wasn't just her business that improved. Her relationships got better, too. After being single for years, Mary started dating again. She said she finally felt confident enough to put herself back in the dating pool. She started attending networking events, where she built relationships with other health and wellness professionals who supported her in her business endeavors and also became her friends. Mary's newfound sense of confidence and belief in herself helped her meet new people and improve her relationships.

You may also notice that you find it easier to get out of your comfort zone and try new things, which is not only fun but also a big part of growth and life satisfaction. You might find yourself wanting to travel somewhere new, try a new hobby or activity, or join a new group or organization. A strong mindset keeps you wanting to try things that will increase your sense of fulfillment.

I often have clients report that their health improves once their mindset improves. They view themselves as stronger, capable, and powerful, which empowers them to make healthy choices for their mind and body. A positive mindset can lead to increased physical movement, healthy choices around food, better stress management, digestive ease, improved self-care, and a better relationship with your body and self-image.

Mindset isn't just about being successful—it's about being *authentically successful*. Cultivating a mindset of authentic success will open you up to a better way of thinking and living – in nearly every area of life.

Chapter 2 Recap:

1. We all have negative thoughts that hold us back from reaching our full potential. Identify the five or 10 negative thoughts that repeat themselves most often in your mind.

2. For each of your negative thoughts, come up with a reframe by completing the following sentences:

    - A more positive way of seeing this is....
    - That's not totally true because....
    - A more powerful way to reframe this thought would be....

3. Determine your three Power Statements by choosing the reframes that feel the most powerful and personal to you.

4. Integrate your Power Statements into your daily life by writing them down somewhere you can see regularly and saying them out loud to yourself daily.

Discovering Your Authentic Style

"The privilege of a lifetime is to become who you truly are." – Carl Jung, Swiss psychologist

Anna was 33 years old and a senior analyst at a prestigious financial firm in Boston. It was the first job she accepted out of college, and she had been there for 10 years. She worked her way up, earning loyalty, appreciation, and steady salary increases as her role at the company elevated. On paper, her life looked perfect. She was making multiple six figures, went on international vacations twice a year, and was well-respected by her colleagues. Outside of her professional life, Anna seemed to be thriving as well. Her husband was a successful attorney, and they had just bought their first home in an up-and-coming suburb of Boston. They were excited to start trying to have children. Her family down in Florida beamed with pride when they talked about Anna and all her success.

But what other people couldn't see was that Anna was *really* struggling.

She woke up each morning and dreaded going to work. She narrowly avoided panic attacks on her commute to work several mornings. Once she arrived at the office, she held her breath and forced herself to complete work she found unenjoyable. The work that once challenged her now felt boring and monotonous. Spreadsheets and market analyses were not enough to excite her. Worst of all, she was doing a *lot* of it, staying late several nights a week to finish tasks with tight deadlines.

When Anna first reached out to me about career coaching, she was looking for a life raft. She was in way too deep with the financial firm, and she couldn't see a way out, but she knew something needed to change.

Anna had always been the creative type. She minored in Art History in college, but her parents had "strongly encouraged" (well, *forced*) her to major in Business Economics so she'd have more job opportunities after graduation. The walls of Anna's new house were adorned with paintings she created in her spare time and photographs taken during her international travels. She'd been attending monthly art classes but often canceled or no-showed due to a work "crisis" or change of plans.

After a few coaching sessions, Anna admitted she was at a crossroads in her career. She knew something needed to change but didn't know what. The job she had taken out of college was her first offer, and it was lucrative and promising at the time. Fast-forward 10 years, and she had become miserable, unfulfilled, and stuck. The weight of her next career move left Anna emotionally paralyzed and increasingly anxious about her future. While her husband made good money, they had just taken on a huge mortgage and were hoping to grow their family. Anna felt that now wasn't the time for a bold leap of faith into a new industry or job.

Anna's predicament was the result of inauthenticity. Despite her passion for art and creative endeavors, she took a job in finance to meet her family's expectations, attain a comfortable salary, and because it was the "easy" choice for a young college graduate. It was never authentically Anna, and the mismatch between her values and her reality led to a mid-career crisis.

If Anna's situation sounds familiar, that's because it happens ALL the time (I see stuff like this every week). As humans, we tend to be drawn to situations and careers that have some external allure – things like money, power, respect, or family approval. The problem is that oftentimes these careers are out of alignment with who you truly are. That means your work doesn't allow you to live in a way that feels authentic to you.

At first, Anna didn't understand that she was living inauthentically. She thought she had a lousy job in a cutthroat industry, and that was her lot in life. That was certainly part of it, but once we dove deeper, Anna realized that her job didn't align with her values, strengths, communication style, and passions. She felt a huge sense of dissatisfaction because she wasn't leveraging her authentic style on a daily basis.

Do you feel dissatisfied in your daily life? Are you:

- Self-censoring: Do you watch what you say in work meetings or social situations, feeling like you can't express your true thoughts or opinions?
- Suppressing creativity: Do you have innovative ideas but you don't act on them (maybe they don't align with the "way things are done" in your current setup)?
- Having value-based inner conflicts: Are you regularly making decisions that go against your personal values to meet job requirements or expectations?
- Neglecting passions: Do you prioritize work over personal hobbies or interests that excite or fulfill you?
- Experiencing relationship inauthenticity: Are you maintaining friendships, romantic relationships, or professional relationships that don't align with who you truly are because you don't want to be alone or feel like you can't say "no" to such people?
- Hiding emotions: Are you suppressing your true feelings or "putting on a good face" to avoid conflict or maintain a professional demeanor?

If you answered **yes** to any of the questions above, I would bet that you aren't living your life 100 percent authentically.

Discovering your authentic style and *living it* on a daily basis will be a game-changer for you. You'll feel happier, more satisfied with your life, and – ultimately – you'll be more successful in your personal and professional pursuits. Authentic living comes with a sense of freedom and fulfillment.

Inauthenticity can permeate your daily life and leave you feeling discontent and stressed. This chapter is all about discovering YOUR authentic style. What are your passions, values, identity, communication style, and behaviors? Let's answer those questions and create a path toward authenticity and connection with your true self.

Foundations of Your Authentic Style

Your authentic style is the genuine expression of who you are.

Your style encompasses your values, strengths, communication style, behavior, decision-making, and even appearance. It's a unique combination of traits, characteristics, and preferences that align with your core identity and remain consistent across various contexts.

An authentic style isn't about being perfect and predictable 100 percent of the time. It's about consistently expressing yourself in a genuine way that feels natural and sustainable to you.

There's an interplay between your values, identity, and behavior:

- **Values:** We discussed core values in Chapter 1. These are the principles and beliefs that guide your decisions, actions, words, and daily priorities. Your values might've been passed down to you by your parents, developed during your formative years, or adopted as you experienced significant changes in your life. Your values play a key part in your identity.

- **Identity:** Your identity is who you are. This is your background, experiences, self-concept, and personality. Your identity is often shaped by your values. If a big shift happens in your life and your values shift, it's likely that your sense of identity will shift as well. Your identity guides your behavior.

- **Behavior:** This is how you act and express yourself in different situations. Your behavior is influenced by your values and your identity. Your behavior also reinforces both your values and identity. For example, consistently acting with integrity in tough situations at work will strengthen your value of integrity and your identity as an ethical leader.

Your values shape your identity, and your identity informs your behavior to define your authentic style. If you need to revisit your top Core Values from Chapter 1 and jot them down so you remember them as you read the rest of this chapter, now is a great time to do that. You're probably already starting to clearly see that your values lay the foundation for many things in your life.

Personal Strengths and Talents

How would you respond if I asked you, "What are your greatest strengths and talents?"

Most of the women whom I coach are at least somewhat aware of their unique gifts, but don't quite know how to articulate them. This is especially true in situations when you have to advocate for yourself or sell yourself. I had one client tell me she was uncomfortable talking about her strengths because it made her feel "braggadocious," which was difficult for her.

Articulating your personal strengths and talents enables you to be more successful, fulfilled, and confident. Your strengths are what make you unique and allow you to make valuable contributions at work and at home. Expressing your personal strengths and talents empowers you to make career and life decisions with these strengths in mind and choose paths that naturally align with these gifts.

Let's further explore your strengths and passions with a coaching exercise I use with my clients. We're going to create two lists in the two-column chart below.

On the left side, create a list of "Things I'm Good at Doing." As you create your list, write down things you consider to be your skills, strengths, and talents. These could be things you're good at professionally or things you're good at doing in your personal time. They can be hard skills (like financial reporting, computer programming, and copywriting) or soft skills (like conflict resolution, time management, and empathy).

On the right side, you'll create a list of "Things I Love to Do." You'll create this list with things you enjoy doing, feel passionate about, or are highly interested in. Once again, these can be specific things at work you enjoy or things you love doing in your personal life.

Don't just do this exercise in your head. Actually, put pen to paper and write down your two lists.

Things I'm Good at Doing:	Things I Love to Do:

Compare the lists and look for items that appear on both sides. Are your lists completely different, or is there overlap? Ideally, your career and the role that you're in would incorporate items from both lists—things you love to do <u>and</u> things you're good at doing.

When my client, Anna, completed this exercise, one item that was on **both** sides of her chart was *creative thinking.* However, so much of her work at the financial firm was analytical and process-oriented and left little room for creativity or innovation. She was good at data analysis (listed on the left side of her chart), but it was NOT something she loved to do. She told me that she aspired to have a job that would allow her to leverage her creative side, but she didn't know where to start and felt pigeonholed in her financial analyst role.

Do your lists have items that appear on both sides? Is there any overlap? Do those items show up in your career on a daily basis? If so, your job will likely be fulfilling and sustainable in the long term. If not, achieving authentic success is unlikely. If your passions and strengths don't align in your career, you'll either not reach the level of success you are truly capable of OR you'll find success, but it will feel unsatisfying and unfulfilling, just like Anna felt at her financial firm.

If you're having trouble identifying some of your strengths, skills, or talents, here are a few questions to get the juices flowing:

- What activities or tasks do you find yourself doing where you lose track of time and feel energized?
- Thinking about your past accomplishments, what are three achievements you're most proud of, and why?
- If you asked your closest friends or colleagues your top three strengths, what would they say?
- What activities or subjects did you naturally excel at or enjoy the most as a kid?
- When you look at your past performance evaluations or feedback, what positive patterns do you notice?
- When you receive compliments, what specific qualities are most often praised?

Many people will tell you to follow your passions and build your career around them, but passion alone isn't enough. It might sound simple and obvious, but it's a powerful reminder: **your career should be something that you enjoy <u>and</u> are good at.** If you're trying to do something you're really bad at, you won't find success—no matter how much you love it. If you're trying to do something that you really hate, you'll be miserable no matter how great you are at it. Find something you enjoy <u>and</u> are good at where you can continue to improve your skills over time. Investing your time and energy at this nexus will bring you satisfaction, fulfillment, and wealth in the long run.

Anna and I came back to her chart several times during her coaching program. Through many conversations, she realized her work needed to involve something more creative for her to feel fulfilled and that she was in alignment with her authentic style.

Anna did not quit her full-time salaried job to become an artist. After careful consideration and planning, Anna proposed to her company that she switch teams within the organization. After some back-and-forth negotiation, she made a lateral move to the marketing department. In her new role, Anna now leads marketing analytics initiatives, applying her mathematical acumen to marketing metrics. She uses her analytical skills from finance to interpret data but also gets to brainstorm creative marketing strategies, combining her logical and artistic sides. She works with various marketing teams, providing guidance on creating visual content for marketing materials and shaping the company's visual and conceptual brand.

In her new role, Anna doesn't have as many tight deadlines, so she feels a lot less pressure. She no longer works late evenings or has "hair on fire" moments during her workdays. She has the time and energy to attend more art classes each month and enjoys her life outside of work much more since her stress is lower.

If you feel like your current role is out of alignment with your authentic style, you might need to make a change like Anna did. You might need a dramatic move like quitting your job and starting over in your career, or it could be a more subtle shift, like a change within your organization.

Let's pause here for a quick check-in. In the box below, write one or two sentences about how you could combine "What I'm Good at Doing" and "What I Love to Do" to make your career authentically successful. Don't overthink it, just write the first thing that comes to mind:

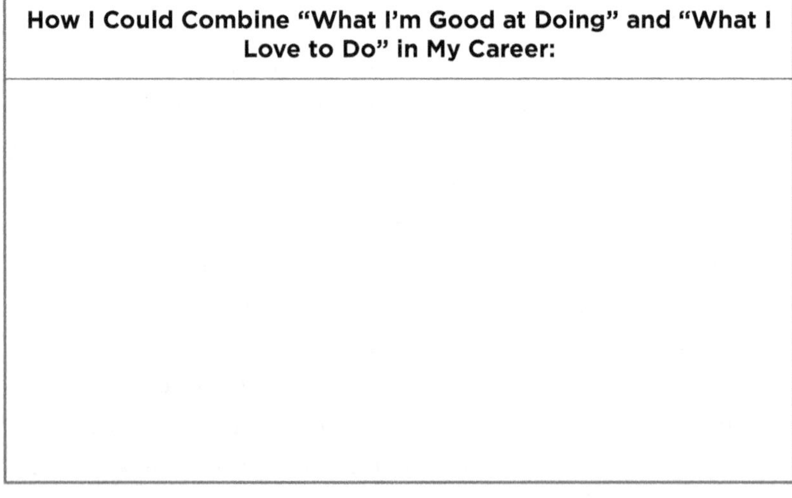

How I Could Combine "What I'm Good at Doing" and "What I Love to Do" in My Career:

Understanding Your Natural Communication Style

Have you ever been talking to another person and felt like you're both speaking English but having entirely different conversations?

I see this all the time with my coaching clients. Recently, Sarah, a software engineer, was frustrated with her boss because he never gave her clear direction. Sarah preferred detailed, specific instructions, while her boss tended to communicate in broad concepts and metaphors. In their meetings, he'd talk about "blue sky thinking" and "pushing the envelope," while Sarah sat there wishing he would just tell her exactly what he wanted her to do. They were both speaking English, but their communication styles were worlds apart.

This kind of communication mismatch happens every day. Whether it's a colleague who emails you a novel when you would prefer a few quick bullet points, or a friend who wants to process everything verbally when you'd rather quietly think through things, differences in communication styles can lead to frustration, misunderstandings, and missed opportunities.

Understanding your own natural communication style—and understanding how to identify others' communication styles—is an important part of achieving authentic success. Communication drives relationships and relationships drive success. When you know how to communicate authentically and adapt that style while staying true to yourself, you become more effective in every interaction—with your colleagues, your family, and your social circle.

When it comes to communication, there are different styles:

Logical vs. Emotional

A logical communicator uses facts, data, and analytics to support her point, while an emotional communicator is feelings-focused and speaks based on gut feelings or intuition.

Direct vs. Indirect

A direct communicator gets straight to the point without sugarcoating anything, while an indirect communicator is more diplomatic and tight-lipped in the way she speaks.

Fast-paced vs. Methodical

A fast-paced communicator thinks fast, talks fast, and makes quick decisions, while a methodical communicator speaks more slowly and takes time to weigh her options before making a decision.

Formal vs. Informal

A formal communicator emphasizes professionalism, tradition, and formality in the way she communicates and often uses official channels of communication (like email or a company Slack channel), while an informal communicator discusses work in a more relaxed context.

Detail-oriented vs. Big Picture

A detail-oriented communicator prefers specificity, details, and step-by-step instructions, while a big-picture communicator prefers broad concepts, big ideas, and inspired (but potentially vague) communication. My client, Sarah, from the beginning of this chapter, is a detail-oriented communicator, while her boss is big picture.

Reserved vs. Expressive

A reserved communicator is more restrained, controlled, and reflective in the way she interacts with others, while an expressive communicator makes her thoughts and feelings easily known and is more open to others.

And the list goes on!

One communication style isn't better than another, but there are situations that warrant using one communication style over others.

How do you communicate in your daily life? Do you know your natural communication style and communication preferences? If not, here are some questions that can help you better understand your communication style:

Questions:	Mark Your Response for Each:
How do you write your emails?	☐ Long-winded ☐ Concise
How do you approach meetings?	☐ I speak up ☐ I prefer to stay quiet
What is your comfort level with conflict?	☐ I avoid conflict ☐ I don't mind ruffling some feathers

How do you give and receive feedback?	☐ I get straight to the point ☐ I sugarcoat
Your preferred method of communication?	☐ Written ☐ Verbal
What's your natural response in high-pressure situations?	☐ I respond quickly ☐ I step back and take time to analyze

Understanding your natural communication style impacts authentic success in powerful ways.

It allows you to lead with your strengths. When you know your natural tendencies—whether you're diplomatic while handling challenging situations or analytical when making financial decisions—you can leverage these traits instead of fighting against them. For example, if you're naturally a detail-oriented communicator like Sarah, you might excel at writing comprehensive SOPs or project documentation. Rather than trying to become more "big picture" because someone told you to, embrace your detail-oriented nature while learning to adjust it depending on the context.

Leading with your style can be a huge leadership advantage. For example:

- Direct communicators often excel at giving feedback
- Indirect communicators often excel at building consensus
- Analytical communicators often excel at project planning
- Emotional communicators often excel at team motivation

Based on the communication style you determined above, what is your leadership advantage? Write it down in the box below:

What leadership advantage does YOUR communication style confer on you?

Awareness of your natural communication style allows you to navigate challenging situations more easily and intentionally. When you know your natural communication style, you can consciously adapt to another style based on the situation at hand. Tailoring the way you communicate with someone depending on the context is a strategy you can use to communicate better and get the outcome you want.

Consider salary negotiations. If you know you're naturally an indirect communicator, you can practice specific direct language and phrases you want to use during your negotiation. Being aware of your indirect communication style, you can practice being more direct and advocating for yourself (which might feel unnatural to you). You're not changing who you are. You're adapting your natural style for better results... which is only possible with this level of self-awareness.

Adapting your natural communication style helps you strengthen your relationships. You can better explain yourself to other people and show them who you are. Instead of forcing yourself to be someone you're not, you're tailoring and adapting your style to meet other people where they are. Know your audience, and get on their level!

People like to be communicated with in their natural style. If you're an emotional communicator and you have a colleague who is more logical, think of ways you can adapt your communication style to meet them where they are. Maybe you bring facts and data that support your points to your next meeting with them. Find ways to adapt while maintaining your authenticity. This will reduce friction in your relationships, build trust, and increase your confidence in both personal and professional interactions.

The goal isn't to *change* who you are but to understand your natural style—and to know how to leverage it and adapt it. This understanding becomes a tool for authentic success rather than a barrier.

Imagine that a direct communicator and an indirect communicator are discussing whether or not to move forward with a new marketing campaign. The direct person says, "This campaign isn't going to work. Our budget is too small and we don't have enough time," while the indirect person says, "This is an interesting concept, but I'm curious how we'd handle the budget and timeline. What are your thoughts on those pieces?" Same message (the campaign isn't feasible), but different delivery—and potential for misunderstanding. The direct communicator might think the indirect person is on board and just asking questions. The indirect communicator might think they clearly expressed concern and expect the team to pivot. Neither realizes they're not on the same page until it's too late.

Misunderstandings like this can lead to unnecessary conflict, slow decision-making, and potentially damaged relationships. Nobody wants this stuff!

Instead, understanding the differences in communication styles and bridging the gap helps you avoid unnecessary stress and drama. You'll anticipate potential misunderstandings, adapt your communication when needed, and ultimately have stronger relationships with the people you spend the most time with, personally and professionally.

Identifying the communication styles of the people you interact with regularly is a powerful advantage. I often work with my clients on "managing "up"—understanding their boss' communication style. If your boss prefers brief bullet-point updates, while you naturally provide lengthy detailed reports, you can adapt while staying authentic. How? You could prepare a summary of your report (with brief bullet points), while also having detailed information ready if further questions are asked.

My client, Leah, came to me feeling frustrated, underappreciated, and dissatisfied at work. Her boss, Cheryl, seemed to give her the cold shoulder. She felt unheard and unseen. While the quality of Leah's work was solid, there were disconnects in her relationships with her colleagues and she couldn't pinpoint exactly what was wrong.

Leah and I worked together to identify her communication style. Her natural style was emotional, direct, and expressive. She provided detailed updates, told stories to illustrate her point, and shared her thoughts and feelings openly. In contrast, Cheryl was more formal and reserved, preferring concise, structured communication. Leah always felt like Cheryl was holding her cards close to her chest, never wanting to speak too much or give herself away. Leah felt like they couldn't form a genuine connection, which she knew would stifle her growth at the company, and this made her uncomfortable.

As we dug deeper into these different communication styles, Leah had a powerful revelation. She realized that her tendency to interrupt during conversations (a product of her expressive nature) was annoying to Cheryl. Her emotional, detailed communication style clashed with Cheryl's preference for brevity and formality. There were certain situations where Leah's enthusiasm and expressiveness, while authentic to her, was creating problems in her relationship with her boss.

With this new awareness, Leah created a plan to intentionally adapt her communication with Cheryl. Her plan looked like this:

- Practice being more concise in meetings (don't ramble)
- Resist the urge to interrupt
- Deliver updates and information in a more structured, succinct way

These weren't fundamental changes to who Leah was. Instead, they were conscious adaptations that allowed her authentic style to work better with Cheryl's preferences.

The results were pretty incredible. Within weeks, Leah's relationship with Cheryl improved. She received more positive feedback and recognition for her work. She felt Cheryl's overall demeanor start to thaw. And most importantly, Leah finally felt heard. By understanding and adapting to her boss' communication style, Leah turned her challenging situation into a productive partnership.

Navigating Team Dynamics

When you have a bunch of different personalities and communication styles working on a team together, it's natural for people to butt heads. There might be one person who talks the loudest and dominates the conversation. Another person may be extremely quiet and introverted, but does great work and you wish they'd speak up more. There might be someone who is passive-aggressive or someone who is just plain aggressive. Maybe there's someone who is always late or rarely shows up at all.

You could have a different communication style for each member of the team.
That isn't a bad thing! In fact, the *best* teams are the ones that make
a variety of styles work well together. High-functioning teams are
well-rounded, have diverse perspectives, and allow different types of
people to contribute according to their strengths. This creates better
team outcomes.

When it comes to working with your team, I recommend checking
your ego at the door. Just because someone communicates differently
than you—or does a lot of things differently than you—doesn't mean
their way is worse or better than yours. Become aware of your own authentic style, and try to get to know your colleagues better so you can
understand their styles, preferences, and values. This means asking
questions, listening—really **listening—when** they speak, and observing how they respond in tough situations. Make a point to listen to learn,
rather than just waiting for your turn to talk. Become more aware of your
teammates' styles and how they are similar to or different from your own.

Practical Suggestions for Navigating Team Dynamics:

- **Build team communication awareness.** Ask team members how
  they like to receive and provide feedback, their ideal meeting format, or how they like to process information. This awareness can
  help avoid misunderstandings and build stronger connections.

- **Adapt to different team members.** If you know that Jenna prefers
  written documentation while Jeff processes information better
  through verbal discussion, you can communicate with them
  in their preferred format. This isn't about changing your style
  completely or changing the message. It's about being thoughtful
  and making adjustments that help information flow smoothly.

- **Create inclusive team environments.** Different styles should
  be welcomed and appreciated since they lead to better team
  outcomes. Create opportunities for different styles to succeed.
  For example, making sure that team meetings don't just cater to
  the most outspoken members of the group. Create opportunities
  for quieter team members to speak up, such as by inviting round-
  robin input on topics.

- **Establish team communication norms.** Work with your team to come up with expectations for how to best communicate with each other. This might include how quickly team members should respond to messages or emails, what communication channels to use for different types of information, how to structure team meetings to accommodate different styles, and guidelines for giving and receiving feedback.

The goal isn't to make everyone communicate in the same way. The goal is to create a productive and cooperative environment where different styles can leverage each other's strengths so the team works together cohesively.

Your Authentic Style Self-Assessment

Now that we've gone over various components of your authentic style—your values, identity, beliefs, and communication preferences—let's pull everything together with a self-assessment. Like the other exercises in this book, don't just do this exercise in your head—actually pick up a pen or pencil and complete the assessment on paper.

Part 1: Core Elements Review	Your top two core values (from Chapter 1): 1. 2. Things you're good at AND things you love to do (items that appear on both sides of your chart from earlier in this chapter): • • • Your natural communication preferences: • • • Your behavioral tendencies: • • •

Part 2: Reflection Questions	**Style Expression:** • Where/when do you feel most authentically yourself? • In what situations do you feel you have to wear a mask? • What aspects of your personality do you tend to hide at work?
	Communication: • How do you naturally express yourself when comfortable? • What communication situations cause you stress? • What feedback have you received from others about your communication style?
	Decision-Making: • How do you like to make important decisions? • What role do emotions play in your decision-making? • What's your natural approach to problem-solving?
	Professional Impact: • What strengths are you currently leveraging at work? • Which parts of your authentic style feel suppressed? • What would your ideal work environment look and feel like?
Part 3: Action Planning	I want to express my authentic style more fully in these specific areas of my life: • • • Situations in which I want to adapt my style include: • • • My specific goals for implementing these changes are: 1. 2. 3.

Discovering and embracing your authentic style is an ongoing journey. The insights from this self-assessment serve as a foundation for taking action and making choices that align with who you truly are.

From Awareness to Action

You've done a lot of self-reflection work in this chapter. You've identified your strengths, what you love to do, how you naturally communicate, and how you show up in different situations. That's powerful self-awareness that most people never take the time to uncover.

This awareness is great, but it's meaningless without *action*.

The real magic happens when you start applying what you've learned. You need to make decisions that align with your authentic style. How do you actually bring this into your life? Start by looking for alignment **and** misalignment.

Go back to your "Things I'm Good At" and "Things I Love To Do" lists from earlier in the chapter. Now think about your current job, your daily tasks, your relationships. Where do you see overlap? Where are you spending time on things that drain you or don't play to your strengths? Those areas of misalignment are where change needs to happen.

You don't have to blow up your life or quit your job tomorrow. But you can start making intentional shifts:

- Can you delegate or reduce tasks that fall outside your strengths?
- Can you volunteer for projects that align with what you love?
- Can you have a conversation with your manager about reshaping your role?
- Can you set boundaries around the things that deplete your energy?

Small, intentional shifts add up to big transformation over time.

There's one more layer to this that I want you to think about: purpose.

Your strengths tell you what you're good at. Your passions tell you what lights you up. But your purpose is where those two things meet a need in the world. It's the intersection of what you do well, what you love, and what makes a difference.

Think of it like this:

- Passion = What you love to do
- Strength = What you're good at
- Purpose = How you use your passion and strength to contribute to something bigger than yourself

You don't need to have your purpose perfectly figured out right now. As you move through the rest of this book and read about building habits, expanding your network, developing mentorship relationships, keep asking yourself: *How can I use who I authentically am to make a meaningful impact?*

That's where authentic success lives. Not just in knowing yourself, but in living as yourself.

Chapter 3 Recap:

1. Your authentic style is the genuine expression of who you really are. It encompasses your strengths, values, communication style, and behaviors. When you live and work in alignment with your authentic style, you'll be more successful and more fulfilled.

2. Understanding your strengths and passions is crucial for success. Complete the exercise "Things I'm Good at Doing" vs. "Things I Love to Do" and identify items that overlap. These are the areas in which you're most likely to thrive professionally.

3. Your natural communication style deeply impacts your personal and professional relationships. While no style is better or worse than another, understanding your style and learning to adapt to the people around you are key to building strong relationships and achieving authentic success.

4. Teams are stronger when they have diverse communication styles and perspectives– but only when those differences are understood and navigated intentionally. Start practicing the strategies for navigating team dynamics outlined in this chapter.

5. Complete the Authentic Style Self-Assessment at the end of this chapter and use it to start guiding your actions toward aligning your life choices with who you truly are.

If you are looking for a tool to help you better understand your unique style, we offer DISC Assessments at www.shatteredglasscoaching.com. The DISC Assessment:

- Helps you discover your unique communication style based on science, revealing exactly how you naturally interact, influence, and collaborate, so you can leverage your innate strengths.
- Provides data-driven insights into your communication preferences and ideal work environments where you'll feel energized and truly thrive.
- Helps you develop the confidence to show up authentically in job interviews, negotiations, and leadership roles, turning your unique style into a powerful career asset.

As a valued reader, you're getting a 50 percent discount off the regular price. Use the QR below to claim your discount and take the DISC Assessment.

Chapter 4

Taking Authentic Action: From Goals to Reality

"Do not wait; the time will never be 'just right.' Start where you stand, and work with whatever tools you may have at your command, and better tools will be found as you go along." – Napoleon Hill, American speaker and author of *Think and Grow Rich*

By this point in the book, you've achieved more than an ordinary person would. You've explored the values, desires, goals, and thoughts within you. Many people live blissfully unaware of these things and instead choose to distract themselves with social media, Netflix shows, or other diversions. It would be easier than facing what's within you. But instead, you've chosen to do the hard work of discovering your authentic style. Kudos for making it this far.

This new awareness of your goals, vision, and style is an important foundation to achieving authentic success. Awareness always precedes action. **Without taking action on this awareness, you're just sitting on a pile of potential.**

This chapter is about taking authentic action. We'll dive into how to make the transition from knowing your style to taking action to make your goals a reality. Identifying concrete actions, habits, and routines will help you get what you really want, both personally and professionally. You'll get clear on your specific next steps and develop a system for making these steps inevitable in your daily life.

The Power of Habits in Authentic Success

In his bestselling book *Atomic Habits*, James Clear states, "The quality of our habits determines the quality of our life." It's a simple statement, but the implications are profound. If you look at someone's daily habits—those actions they repeat, often subconsciously—it tells you a lot about who that person is and what their life is like!

Let's talk about Lisa. In my 20s, Lisa was my charismatic, talkative coworker who was often cracking jokes and making the office laugh. As I spent more time working with Lisa and getting to know her better, I started picking up on some of her habits. I noticed that she:

- Shopped online often
- Ate fast food for almost every meal
- Watched Netflix for several hours each night
- Didn't "believe in" exercising (she used to joke about this)
- Bought Beanie Babies online that she hoped to resell on eBay (but usually didn't)

Individually, there might not be anything wrong with these habits. As I worked with Lisa longer and learned more about her on a personal level, I saw her struggling with her health, her finances, and her overall happiness in life. She was often sick and absent from work, going to the doctor. She was very vocal about her credit card debt but would easily spend $1,000 in one day doing online shopping. Behind the funny, personable coworker we all loved, I had a feeling she was really hurting.

It's been more than 10 years since I've worked with Lisa, but she recently posted on social media that she has a chronic health condition related to her lifestyle and that she filed for bankruptcy. I have empathy for Lisa and have always wished her well, but I wasn't at all surprised when I learned about her recent news. The habits that I observed all those years ago were clues to something bigger (and unhealthier) going on in her life. Those early habits have manifested as her present condition.

Now let's talk about Jen. Jen was a potluck roommate I had in California, and living together meant I got to know her quickly. It didn't take long for me to see that Jen was consistent and self-disciplined in how she lived her life. After living with her for just a couple of months, here are her habits that I noticed. She:

- Woke up early and took a two- or three-mile walk before work every day
- Read books that enriched her mind most evenings (usually self-development, educational, or financial books)
- Jogged consistently and went to "run club" twice weekly
- Hiked with friends on the weekends
- Cooked healthy, homemade meals
- Participated in professional development activities like conferences, courses, and additional trainings
- Spent frugally, but would invest in high-quality, long-lasting clothing

Jen seemed generally satisfied with her life. While it certainly wasn't perfect, she enjoyed taking care of herself and developing herself within her career while spending time with friends and planning for her future.

We no longer live together, but I also keep up with Jen on social media. She's been promoted multiple times at work and has won awards at her company. She travels internationally several times a year for pleasure, runs marathons regularly, and has a tight-knit group of friends she spends a lot of time with. She is *thriving*! And you know what? I was not at all surprised by this. The habits I saw in Jen when we lived together all pointed to a full, healthy, and successful life.

I don't compare Lisa and Jen to be judgy. I compare them because they are clear examples of how your habits shape your daily life and, over time, the longer-term outcomes in your life. The little things you do routinely really do make a difference in your quality of life and long-term success.

Your habits are more than just your repeated behaviors. They are daily declarations of your beliefs and values. When your habits are aligned with your authentic self, you're not just going through the motions. You're living in harmony with yourself.

Think about it. If you value creativity but never make time for creative pursuits, there's a disconnect between the life you want and the life you have. If you say you value health and wellness, but your habits undermine your health and well-being, you're not living in alignment with your authentic self.

Your habits either reinforce or oppose your authentic self.

Bad habits <u>oppose</u> your authentic self. When you:

- Check Instagram first thing in the morning, you're developing a habit of external stimulation, distraction, or instant gratification
- Skip lunch to keep working, you're creating a habit of putting work above your self-care
- Say "yes" to every request from your boss when you're already at full capacity; you're ignoring your boundaries

Conversely, good habits <u>reinforce</u> your authentic self, which might look like:

- Starting your day with meditation if you value inner peace
- Blocking time for creative work if you value creativity, or exercise if you value fitness
- Setting clear boundaries if you value self-respect

The key is to develop good habits that reinforce your values and support your goals, rather than bad habits that work against you.

Habits are more reliable than motivation. What does "motivation" even mean? Is it when you wake up and magically feel compelled to do something wonderful for yourself, your career, your health, or your life? Is it when you have a moment of inspiration and start a new project? Is it when you see someone else doing something incredible and it makes you want to do it, too?

"Motivation" is a fleeting rush of dopamine; it's not something we're born with. It comes and goes, and we can't keep it in a bottle. If you're sitting around waiting for motivation to propel you toward your goals, you're setting yourself up for failure. Because motivation ebbs and flows, it's not a reliable way to keep you moving forward. Some days you'll have it and other days you won't.

On days that you aren't motivated, your *habits* are what keep you on track. Creating habits for sustaining your progress is exactly what keeps momentum going. Since motivation is fleeting, you need a dialed-in routine you can follow day after day that keeps you moving forward. It's like athletes who say, "I didn't feel like coming to the gym today, but I showed up because that's just what I do." Even after a bad night of sleep or an emotionally tough conversation with a loved one, that athlete is still going to the gym, even if they have zero motivation, because that's a habit they've developed to keep their athletic performance where it needs to be. *Habits trump motivation every time.*

Your Current Habits Assessment

Let's take an honest look at your current habits, both those that are serving you and those that are holding you back from being authentically successful. Grab your pen or pencil and let's dive in.

Complete the assessment below. On the left-hand side, write a list of the habits that are serving you. When you think about your daily and weekly routines, what are the actions or habits that make you feel energized, productive, or aligned with your values? List your positive behaviors here. Your list might include morning habits, work habits, relationship habits, or self-care habits.

On the right-hand side, create a list of the habits that are holding you back. These are the habits that might be preventing you from reaching your full potential or living authentically. This list might include things like doom-scrolling on social media, eating candy late at night, drinking alcohol to cope with stress, or answering work emails at all hours of the night.

Habits Assessment

Habits That Are Serving Me	Habits That Are Holding Me Back

Looking at your assessment above, answer the following reflection questions:

Question:	Your Answer:
Which three habits make you feel MOST energized and fulfilled?	1. 2. 3.
Which three habits leave you feeling MOST drained or inauthentic?	1. 2. 3.
What usually triggers your bad habits?	
What habits do you want to remove from your life?	
What habits do you want to add to your life?	

By completing your **Habits Assessment** and answering the reflection questions above, you've identified the positive habits that already serve you AND the habits you'd like to add to your life. Your next step is creating a plan for incorporating these habits into your daily life.

Building Authentic Habits

Almost half of your day is lived unconsciously! Research by the Society for Personality and Social Psychology shows that 40-50 percent of all actions you take in a day are considered automatic and habitual. Unconscious habits have a huge impact on your decision-making and ultimately the outcomes you see in your life.

Positive habits are the actions that align with your values and support your goals. Making positive habits a consistent and unconscious part of your daily life will lead to bigger changes and outcomes. For example, creating a habit of getting to bed by 9 p.m. each night with the lights off and your phone in the other room (and actually sticking to it!) will result in better-quality sleep, more energy, and likely a better overall mood the next day.

Building a brand-new habit is no easy feat. Your critter brain likes to stick to what is familiar, easy, and safe. A new habit may feel different and challenging, and you'll notice yourself resisting (either consciously or subconsciously). Fortunately, with all the research around habits that's come out in the last decade—and thanks again to *Atomic Habits*—we have a solid understanding of how to build new habits.

The Habit-Building Process:

1. **Start small.** If you add a bunch of new habits into your life all at once, you're setting yourself up for failure. Even if you have a ton of new habits you want to build to overhaul your daily life, I still recommend starting small. Pick a maximum of <u>three habits</u> you'd like to add—the three that would make the biggest difference in your daily life and perhaps even create a domino effect for other habits. Make sure they're realistic, and you have time for them. Let's say you want to create a habit of walking daily, and you're currently not

walking at all. Start with a goal of walking 10 minutes a day, not 60 minutes. After a week of successfully walking 10 minutes daily, increase it to 20 minutes daily. Starting small keeps your habits sustainable and gives you ample time to focus on integrating them into your daily life, rather than aiming too high and setting yourself up to fail. Focus on mastering a habit or two at a time before you start adding more new habits.

2. **Create triggers.** Triggers are cues or catalysts that make an action or habit happen. Triggers make your habits easier to do by signaling your brain to take action. By intentionally setting up triggers in your external environment, you initiate a habit. Waking up and getting out of bed might trigger a morning coffee routine. When you add a *new* habit to your daily routine, set up a trigger to signal yourself to do that habit. This helps make sure you follow through. An easy example of this: If you want to start exercising in the morning, you can lay out your gym clothes and sneakers the night before. Fill up your water bottle and have your car keys laid out beside it. When you wake up and see your gym clothes and sneakers ready to go, it acts as a trigger and tells your brain, "Hey, it's time to get dressed and go to the gym—let's go!"

3. **Track your progress.** Measuring and tracking your progress reinforces consistency over time. *Atomic Habits* suggests using a tool: the habit tracker. The concept is simple. You use a habit tracker to log your habits daily. This means you can track your progress, hold yourself accountable, and make it easy to immediately see how consistent you are with individual habits. You write down the habits you want to complete each day, and then, at the end of the day, you check them off (or put an X, shade in, or use colored pencils) to indicate whether you completed the habit on that day. As time goes on, the habit tracker becomes a clear record of your progress. It's a visual tool that reminds you to act on your habits, providing both motivation and accountability. When you see your "habit streak," you'll want to keep it going. It feels good when you succeed with your

habits! It's satisfying and fun to check off your boxes each day and celebrate your positive habits. There are plenty of habit tracker templates out there. You can find them just by googling "habit tracker."

4. **Maintain consistency.** Research by psychologist Dr. Jeremy Dean shows that, on average, forming a new habit takes 66 days. In those 66 days, being consistent with your new habits is often the most crucial element for success. Consistency does NOT mean perfection; it means getting back on track quickly when you slip up. Think of consistency like steering a ship. You're constantly making small adjustments to stay on course, rather than expecting to move in a perfectly straight line. If you find yourself struggling to remain consistent with one of your new habits, consider scaling back that habit slightly until you find a version of it that's more sustainable.

Breaking Habits That Don't Serve You

Building positive habits will only get you so far. If you have habits in your life that are negative, destructive, misaligned with your values, or that counteract your positive habits, you'll stay stuck. To find authentic success, you need to let go of the habits that aren't serving you.

In your **Habits Assessment** above, you identified habits that are holding you back. It's important to understand why these habits were formed in the first place. You might realize that they aren't all inherently ""bad"—they might be providing useful information you can take and use. For example, one of your negative habits might be that you scroll mindlessly on social media before bed.

Let's consider where that habit came from. It could be that you have trouble falling asleep, and scrolling gives you something to do while you wait to get tired. It could be that you've been working hard all day and your brain wants something mindless and easy to do. It could be that you're lonely before bed, and social media makes you feel (temporarily) more connected to others. Once you understand WHY this habit was formed in the first place, it gives you good information about how to break it or what to do instead.

In his book, *The Power of Habit*, award-winning journalist Charles Duhigg discusses what's known as "Replacement Theory"—it's easier to replace a bad habit than to simply stop it altogether. Let's stick with the example of scrolling social media before bed. You can substitute that negative behavior with something more positive that serves a similar purpose. If the issue is that you have trouble falling asleep, consider replacement habits like reading a book, taking a bath, or having a magnesium drink. If the issue is that you feel lonely before bed, consider replacement habits like calling or texting your friends or family before bedtime to check in and say goodnight.

It's also important to consider how your physical environment impacts your habits. If you can modify your environment to make bad habits more difficult, it can help you stop these negative behaviors. By removing triggers, you can stop the bad habit before it even starts. If you keep your phone out of the bedroom before you go to sleep, it removes the trigger of scrolling before bedtime. While this requires discipline and a commitment to removing your phone from the room, it could be the key to creating an environment that helps you break that bad habit. If you're thinking, "But I use my phone as my alarm clock!"—I hear you. Consider investing in a standalone alarm clock instead. There are some great options out there, like sunrise alarm clocks from Lumie or Philips that wake you up with gradual light instead of a jarring sound. It's a small investment that removes the temptation entirely.

When you break the habits that don't serve you, you're living more authentically. Your habits either reinforce or oppose your authentic self. Since your habits are the daily expressions of who you are and what you value, having bad habits holds you back from being who you truly are. Remind yourself: "I'm becoming someone who..." and embrace the identity of the person who is authentically aligned with your positive habits.

Facing Challenges and Building Resilience

Now that you know which habits you want to adopt and which habits you want to break, you're ready to start implementing them. In 66 days, they'll be automatic and you'll be set for life, right? Unfortunately, it's not exactly *that* easy.

As you start building authentic habits, you will undoubtedly face challenges that will throw you off your game and require you to make adjustments and build self-discipline. When it comes to building new habits, here are some of the most common obstacles I see my coaching clients face:

- **Time constraints:** If you have a demanding career that monopolizes most of your daylight hours, it can be difficult to prioritize new habits. You may also have family obligations and caregiving responsibilities that take priority. Or you might just feel overwhelmed by everything you have on your plate, which puts your new habits on the back burner.

- **Perfectionism:** I hear this from clients ALL the time: "I'm waiting for the perfect time to start." Newsflash: There is <u>never</u> going to be a "perfect" time. This all-or-nothing thinking sets unrealistic expectations and sets you up for failure.

- **Fear or self-doubt:** Do you ever question whether you're "ready" or "qualified" for the life you want? This line of impostor syndrome thinking gets in the way of building positive habits. I regularly hear from clients that they have a fear of failure and self-judgment and self-sabotaging thoughts, which are getting in the way of the life they really want.

- **Lack of support:** If your family members, spouse, colleagues, or closest friend are unsupportive, it makes it difficult to build new habits. You might feel isolated as you pursue your goals.

- **External challenges:** Life happens. You might be having health issues, family emergencies, financial setbacks, or a work crisis. These types of external disruptions can derail your new positive habits.

- **Energy management:** When you're physically, mentally, or emotionally exhausted, it's difficult to build good habits. You might feel stress from your competing priorities or be burnt out from overextending yourself at work. A lack of energy can be a big obstacle standing between you and your habits of success.

While they aren't the most fun things to deal with, these obstacles are part of life. It's ultimately your choice as to how to handle them. Will you allow these obstacles to stop you from building positive habits? Will you revert back to bad habits when one of these obstacles comes up? Or will you have the mental toughness to face these challenges and stick to your values and authentic habits?

Let's talk about mental toughness for a minute. Mental toughness is **not** the same thing as "pushing through" when you need a break. Mental toughness means staying focused, resilient, and confident in the face of challenges, while staying true to your authentic self. It's not about hiding your emotions or ignoring the bad things going on in your life. It's having the inner strength to embrace the challenge and push forward toward your goals, even when faced with obstacles, self-doubt, or setbacks.

Mental toughness doesn't mean you don't feel fear, doubt, or exhaustion. When you feel these things, acknowledge them and move forward anyway, even if only in small ways. It's the bridge between knowing what you want and actually achieving it.

Here are three examples of mental toughness:

1. **When illness strikes:** Amanda committed to morning workouts but got the flu two weeks into her new routine. Instead of letting this derail her completely, she accepted the temporary pause, modified her exercises during recovery, and got back to her usual routine as soon as she was well. She used the setback to build a backup plan for future illnesses.

2. **When work tries to take over your personal life:** Diana was trying to develop a habit of leaving work by 5 p.m. so she could be home in time to have dinner with her kids. When her VP started regularly scheduling 5 p.m. meetings, she showed mental toughness by having a direct and honest conversation with her VP about her schedule, proposing alternative meeting times, setting clear

boundaries while maintaining professionalism, and standing firm on her commitment to leave by 5 p.m.

3. **When you keep getting interrupted:** Sarah worked in an open office environment where she was easily distracted by her coworkers. She was establishing a habit of deep, focused work, but kept getting interrupted. She adapted by creating "do not disturb" signs, blocking focused time on her calendar, finding alternative quiet spaces in the building, and maintaining her concentration practice despite distractions.

One way to develop mental toughness is by intentionally getting out of your comfort zone. *Deliberate discomfort* forces you to do things that, while seeming a bit scary or daunting, will result in personal growth. Eleanor Roosevelt said, "Do one thing every day that scares you." By taking on slightly uncomfortable tasks regularly, you develop grit and resilience over time. If you get nervous when speaking up during work meetings, get out of your comfort zone by making a point to speak up and contribute more in those meetings.

If you typically avoid confrontation because you don't like having difficult conversations with people, practice having those difficult conversations promptly instead of avoiding them. This kind of courage and deliberate discomfort develops your mental toughness and better arms you to handle challenges when they arise.

Reframe your setbacks or challenges as learning opportunities. What lesson is that difficulty trying to teach you about yourself, and how can you learn from it? From there, focus on *progress over perfection*. You don't need to do things perfectly, but making incremental progress in the right direction each week will add up over time. Your challenges are temporary and surmountable—you WILL overcome them. Take time to self-reflect, especially during these difficult times, and develop a growth-oriented mindset that will help you persevere through the challenges.

Creating **recovery plans** is another important part of overcoming setbacks. Since you know setbacks are inevitably going to happen, make a plan for setbacks before they pop up. By having a "bounce back routine," you can hit the reset button when you need to. You might take one hour every Sunday to self-reflect, map out your week ahead, and align with your goals and habits. If the week before was especially challenging and you let your habits slip, this Sunday reset hour would be a great time to recommit to your goals and habits and make a game plan to set you up for success for the week ahead.

When challenges come up, and good habits go out the window, I often hear my clients take themselves on a guilt trip. They beat themselves up for not being consistent or sticking to the plan. This is when I encourage the 48-Hour Rule. Allow yourself to feel disappointed, angry, or upset for 48 hours—process those emotions without dwelling. Cry in the shower, scream into a pillow, vent to your best friend, or journal it out. Then, after 48 hours, shift to solution mode. This is your time to hit "reset" or implement your recovery strategy. Create an action plan for getting back in the driver's seat, without ruminating on time lost or habits missed.

As you're reframing and creating your action plan for moving forward, try to think objectively about where things went wrong. Was it an unusually busy week? Did you get sick? Was there a family crisis? Did you deprioritize your habits for some other reason? After determining the root cause of the problem, reflect on lessons you can learn from the setback. You can adjust your habits or your approach based on these insights.

Let's say you want to make a habit of exercising every morning. However, you find that after not sleeping well, you aren't able to drag yourself out of bed and get to the gym. Instead of saying, "I'm a failure and shouldn't exercise anymore," view this setback as feedback, not failure. You might need to try exercising after work in the evenings. Or maybe you need to focus on dialing in your sleep routine so you're getting some solid Z's and feel refreshed enough to work out in the morning. Rather than beating yourself up or quitting, reflect and make adjustments to your plan based on what went wrong.

From there, keep building your momentum forward! Take immediate positive action, even if it's just a tiny step in the right direction.

Focus on what you **can** control, not what you can't control. Look for ways to create new opportunities, find new successes, and take aligned action. Keep moving forward, even if you feel uncertain.

One of my coaching clients, Alex, wanted to make a habit of going to sleep earlier each night. She liked to go to the gym in the evenings, then eat a late dinner, shower, and unwind for the day by watching Netflix or scrolling through Instagram. She found that most nights she wasn't getting to sleep until 11:30 p.m. or midnight, and she was exhausted in the mornings. We started by drawing boundaries around her evening schedule and timing. She committed to being in bed, lights out, and head on the pillow by 10:30 each night. In order to do this, she decided she probably needed to start "winding down" and getting off screens by 9:30, which would allow her to use that hour to shower and do her nightly skincare routine, have a magnesium drink, and read a fiction book to quiet her mind.

The first week of trying out her new evening habits, Alex had mixed success. There were several nights that she was able to successfully be in bed and off her phone or the TV by 9:30 p.m., so she could wind down and be asleep by 10:30. But there were other nights that she ended up back on her phone scrolling through Instagram until the wee hours of the morning.

After talking it over, Alex and I pinpointed the root cause of the problem: she revealed that she usually slept with her phone sitting on her bed, right next to her pillow. Even when she got in bed at 9:30 with her book and the best intentions to get to sleep on time, if her cell phone would ping with an Instagram notification or a text from a friend, it would totally derail her, and she would go down the Instagram rabbit hole, scrolling until midnight.

With this in mind, I knew we had to adjust Alex's habits. As long as her phone was sitting in her bed, she wouldn't avoid Instagram at night, which would prevent her from forming her new habit of going to sleep at a decent hour. We created a new action plan that would set her up for success.

First, we decided that at 9:30, Alex needed to plug in her phone on the other side of the room – NOT in her bed or even on her nightstand, but *across the room*. This would ensure that she couldn't easily grab her phone from right beside her while winding down. I suggested that Alex also turn on her phone's "do not disturb" feature, which you can automate to turn on at certain times, keeping notifications or calls from distracting her. However, with aging parents, Alex worried that she might miss a call from her sister (her parents' caregiver) if there was an emergency. When Alex learned that you could allow calls from certain phone contacts, even while your phone is in "do not disturb" mode, she felt more comfortable with the plan.

With all this in mind, Alex came up with a new plan of action for her nighttime routine:

- She set an alarm on her phone for 9:30 p.m. daily and labeled it "wind-down hour."
- This alarm cued her to plug in her phone across the bedroom.
- She set up her phone to automatically turn on her "do not disturb" feature to avoid getting notifications from 9:30 p.m. until 7:30 a.m., except for those from her sister, from whom she would still receive calls or texts.
- After her phone was plugged in, Alex showered, had her magnesium drink, and got in bed to do some reading before turning the lights out at 10:30 p.m.

The small tweaks that Alex made to her nighttime routine made a big difference. After making these changes, she consistently met her goal of being asleep by 10:30 every single night the following week. It wasn't magic – it was simply Alex's willingness to persevere and stick to her goals, combined with getting to the source of the problem and making the adjustments to her habits that would set her up for success. By doing something as small as removing her phone from her bed, Alex created a domino effect on the rest of her evening. Being solution-minded and taking time to reflect on what worked and what didn't is what allowed Alex to change her approach and ultimately adopt a new bedtime routine.

From Planning to Doing

Earlier in this chapter, you identified the new habits you wanted to ADD to your life. Now let's move from *planning* to **doing**. Just identifying these new habits and writing them down isn't enough. You need to take strategic action to make them a reality. Let's start by breaking those habits down into actionable steps.

Questions to ask yourself for each habit:

Is this habit realistic?

Remember to start small when building your new habit. Set yourself up for success by being realistic with yourself about what's reasonable, and work your way up from there. If you need to revise your habit, break it down into smaller chunks, or make it smaller and more doable, go for it.

When in my day will I incorporate this habit?

Identify the *exact time* in your day that this habit will take place. If you leave it up to "I'll do it when I have time for it," then you're not planning for success, and it'll slip through the cracks.

What is my trigger for this habit?

A trigger cues you to start a new habit. Make sure you have something in place to signal your brain that it's time to do your habit. If you want to get in the habit of taking daily vitamins, put them right by the coffeemaker. Pouring your coffee in the morning could then become your trigger for taking your vitamins.

How will I track my progress for this habit?

I recommend printing out a Habit Tracker (or using a virtual template) and writing your top three habits there to track them. You can also track your habits in your daily planner, journal, or a habit-tracking app on your phone. Make sure you have a way to visually see or check off your progress.

What are the potential obstacles or challenges I'll have in adopting this new habit?

You know yourself best. Anticipate your potential obstacles in advance so you can have a plan for when they inevitably come up. Do you struggle with time management? Do you not have the financial resources available for a certain habit? Do you have mindset blocks that will hinder you? Write down all the potential things that could go wrong, and then create a game plan for what you'll do when things go sideways. Have it in writing so you can refer back to it and get yourself unstuck when you need to.

Earlier in this chapter, you also identified the habits you wanted to *remove* from your life. These are the habits that you feel are inauthentic and holding you back or draining your energy. Now, let's create a strategic plan of action for getting rid of those habits. For each habit you want to *break*, ask yourself:

Why did I form this habit in the first place?

Bad habits usually stem from something. It could be boredom, the need to unwind after a long day, or your desire to find meaning in meaningless places. Identify the root cause of each of these habits to help you remove the habit from your life.

What can I replace this habit with instead?

It's easier to replace a habit than to remove it altogether. My client, Alex, replaced scrolling on her phone in bed at night with reading a book in bed with her phone plugged in across the room. What can you replace your bad habit with instead?

Do I need to change anything in my physical environment to help me remove this habit?

Your physical environment dramatically impacts your habits. Make modifications to your physical environment that will help set you up for success. If you're trying to break the habit of eating processed sugar, you might remove all sugary foods from your house. Go through the kitchen, pantry, cabinets, and drawers—anywhere these foods might be—and physically remove them from the house. Throw them out or give them away! By removing these foods from your physical environment, you reduce temptation and make it easier to avoid the bad habit altogether.

How will I track my progress for removing this habit?
Just like the three habits you want to add to your life, you can also track and measure progress for the habits you want to break. Full disclosure: "No online shopping" is at the top of my habit tracker because it's a habit I want to break. It feels SO satisfying when I check that box for not online shopping each day. You can do the same for other habits you're trying to break by adding them to your habit tracker.

Creating Accountability

We've already talked about some forms of self-accountability. Your habit tracker, triggers, and physical environment are tools for holding yourself accountable. But sometimes this just isn't enough. Many people are extrinsically motivated and require (or want) some form of external accountability to keep them going.

The American Society of Training and Development (ASTD) conducted a study on accountability and found that you have a 65% chance of completing a goal if you commit to someone. And if you have a specific accountability appointment with a person you've committed to, you will increase your chance of success by up to 95 percent.

I know a lot of people who keep their goals to themselves. They aren't vocal about their weight loss journey, the business they're building, their financial goals, or anything else they want to achieve. Why? I think it's because it puts you in a vulnerable position. Talking about yourself is scary! And if people KNOW you're trying to achieve something—and then you fail—they'll be there to watch you fall flat on your face.

Even though it might feel vulnerable or uncomfortable, saying your goals out loud to friends and family members makes them more <u>real</u>. You speak them to the world, and they become tangible. I once heard a client say, "Well, I told my boss I'm going to run a marathon, so I guess

I have to do it now." The act of articulating it out loud to someone made it more tangible and real for her, thus, the stakes went up. (She did end up actually running the marathon!)

Creating systems for accountability and support is one of the most effective ways to develop new habits and ultimately achieve your goals. *Accountability is the key to success.*

Having a strong support system is also crucial when recovering from a setback. This might look like an impromptu conversation with your partner or a close friend to get you back on the wagon. You might be part of an accountability group or have a trusted coach or mentor who you can talk to. Having the right support system can get you back on track after facing a challenge. In our next chapter, we'll dive deeper into how your relationships fuel your authentic journey.

You don't have to do everything by trial and error. Seek guidance from those who have experience. Maybe they already have what you want. Maybe they've been on some version of your journey and are now on the other side. Maybe they have skills and experience that you yourself don't already have. Find support and accountability from someone who has been there and can help you.

Chapter 4 Recap:

1. Consistent actions become your habits, which shape your life outcomes. The quality of your habits determines the quality of your life. Each small action contributes to your overall success.

2. **Authentic habits** align with your values and support your true self. When your daily actions express what you genuinely believe and value, you're living authentically.

3. Consistency trumps motivation every single time. Since motivation is fleeting, creating sustainable habits is what will keep the momentum going—even on days when you don't feel inspired.

4. Start small, create triggers, track your progress, and maintain consistency. These four steps form the foundation of successful habit-building.

5. Breaking habits requires an understanding of their root cause and the creation of intentional replacements. Modify your environment to make bad habits more difficult and good habits easier.

6. Building mental toughness and resilience helps you overcome inevitable setbacks. Allow yourself to process challenges, then shift to solution mode with a clear action plan.

7. Accountability drastically increases your chances of authentic success. Whether through habit tracking or sharing your goals with others who will support you and give you tough love, creating systems of accountability is crucial to achieving authentic success.

If you haven't already, don't forget that you can download the exercises and worksheets for this book. Scan the QR code below to access them digitally for free.

Human Authenticity
in an AI-Driven World

"Technology is a useful servant but a dangerous master." – Christian Louis Lange, historian and political scientist

I was recently having drinks with a friend, and we were catching up on life, work, and relationships. As we were chatting, she told me a crazy story. She got into an argument with another friend (the details of which are irrelevant) that led to them not speaking to each other for several months. Much to her relief, my friend one day received an apology text message from her friend. It was a multi-paragraph text message that read like a thoughtful apology. However, as soon as my friend got to the bottom of the text message, her heart dropped. The text message ended like this:

Would you like me to adjust this to better reflect your specific situation or a more detailed reason for the gap in communication?

My friend quickly realized that the apology text was AI-generated. Anyone who has used ChatGPT or a similar platform will recognize that final sentence as something that AI spits out after it generates written content for you. Apparently, the apologizer in this situation forgot to remove that last sentence before copying and pasting the AI-written apology.

Obviously, my friend was hurt. Even if the *intention* behind the apology was sincere, the fact that it was written by AI made it come off as phony and inauthentic. As she told me the story, I was astounded. I shared her sense of anger that she was owed a true "I'm sorry" and that the AI words totally negated any real apology. For days after hearing this story from my friend, I couldn't stop thinking about it.

In recent years, there has been an exponential rise in AI-generated content and communication. According to Gallup research, as of mid-2025, about 52 percent of US adults have used large language models (LLMs—advanced text generation systems like ChatGPT and Gemini), and 60 percent interact with them at least several times weekly. It's not just individuals. Corporate use of AI is on the rise, too. Stanford's 2025 AI Index Report found that AI use in companies rose to 78 percent in 2024, a significant increase from 55 percent in 2023. I'm certain it will be much higher than that when the 2025 report comes out and will only increase in future years.

People use AI to help research, brainstorm, proofread, string words together, and generate ideas for personal and professional projects. AI can make people more productive and efficient with their time, and can automate things that may have taken much longer if done manually.

But there's a paradox—these **tools that are meant to help us express ourselves can dilute us instead.** We're using AI to sound more articulate and thoughtful, yet in doing so, we're removing the very humanity that makes communication meaningful.

AI is making people *less authentic* (artificial is literally in the name!). The seemingly thoughtful and carefully written apology text message my friend received actually made her feel **worse** about her connection with her friend. Using AI in this situation, even if the intention was to form a coherent apology, actually broke a human relationship more than it strengthened it by cheapening the effort involved.

As the 21st century is more and more defined by AI, I believe that authentic human connection will matter more than ever before. As our words increasingly come from algorithms rather than our hearts, the value of genuine human expression becomes increasingly more important.

This chapter explores how to maintain your authentic voice in a world where AI-generated content is not just typical but expected.

Understanding the Impact

AI has changed personal and professional communication *for good*. People are starting to substitute AI-generated content for personal expression. This can be seen in work emails, social media captions, creative writing, and even in personal communications with family or friends.

Think about the emails you receive in your inbox on a daily basis. Think about the social media feed you scroll through. A growing number of those emails and social media posts are created by AI, not human writers. SQ Magazine reported that 71 percent of images shared on social media are now AI-generated. And on LinkedIn, roughly 54 percent of long-form posts are likely created by AI.

The widespread use of AI for communication raises questions about authenticity. But let's go back to the paradox. People use AI because they want to leverage a tool to help them express themselves more clearly and effectively. They want to sound more like themselves but actually end up sounding less authentic. There's a huge disconnect between polished AI content and genuine human expression. It's usually easy to pick up on! I'm sure you've seen that beautifully crafted email that uses the "right words" and says all the "right things," but something about it just sounds off... like maybe a robot wrote it? Perhaps it's the use of words or phrases that humans just don't typically use, or it's attempting humor in a way a human writer probably wouldn't, or it has an odd sentence structure. Recipients of AI-written content can often sense when communication lacks genuine human touch, even when the AI has done a "good job."

What's even more concerning to me is how people's reliance on AI may diminish their own communication skills. The loss of personal writing style or voice will quickly erode our authenticity. I think about younger people who might be in college or just beginning their career journey. Relying on AI from a young age will preclude these young professionals from ever developing their authentic voice.

Before we go fully down the "AI = Doomsday" spiral, let's acknowledge the difference between *enhancement* and *replacement*. Using AI to refine your ideas is different than having it create content for you.

Utilizing AI for things like editing, research assistance, and idea organization is a great way to leverage AI without losing your authentic voice. When it comes to generating personal messages, creative expression, and emotional content, AI can't replace your authentic self. Using AI thoughtfully and intentionally can help you make your communication more human, but delegating your content creation to AI entirely will destroy your authenticity.

Here are signs your authentic voice might be getting lost in AI:

- You can't write without AI assistance.
- You feel like your own writing doesn't sound "good enough."
- You're uncomfortable sending unedited emails or messages.
- You share AI-generated content as if it's your own.
- You're having trouble articulating original thoughts in real-time situations.
- You're generally over-relying on AI.

As AI-generated content is becoming more ubiquitous, authenticity becomes more valuable.

In a crowd of algorithmic content, an authentic human connection stands out! It's what makes you unique, genuine, magnetic, and successful. Literally anyone can hop online and use ChatGPT to spit out something that sounds polished and brilliant. But not everyone can use their authentic voice to connect and make a difference. There is a growing premium being placed on human creativity and authentic expression – it's time to embrace it.

Being authentically "you" builds trust with the people you interact with, both personally and professionally. Humans fundamentally crave genuine connection, and that is exactly what has been lost in the rise of AI. Research has shown that authentic communication improves outcomes across contexts and industries. One study by BMC Health Services Research found that authentic communication between patients and their providers improved health outcomes among older patients. When patients in this study had authentic relationships with their providers, it:

- Enhanced patients' trust in their providers
- Improved social, somatic, and psychological health
- Strengthened patients' perception of control over their health
- Contributed to patients' positive experiences, like shorter hospital stays

This study highlights a universal truth that extends beyond the healthcare industry: In a world increasingly dominated by AI-generated content, the human ability to communicate with authenticity is an advantage that confers measurable, tangible benefits that no algorithm can replicate.

In the era of AI, finding and maintaining your authentic voice makes you irreplaceable. There are human qualities within you that AI can *never replace*:

Intuition.

Empathy.

Lived experience.

Even as AI advances in future years, it's important to continue cultivating your own unique perspective and voice, future-proofing your value, and making you authentically successful.

Finding Your Authentic Voice

In Chapter 3, we identified your authentic communication style. This is your unique way of communicating with others based on your background, life experiences, and personality. These all shape how you naturally express yourself. Just like every human has different DNA, your communication style is as unique as your fingerprint. I often hear from clients and friends who are struggling to find their voice or express themselves authentically, especially in professional contexts.

Here's a quick assessment you can do right now to gain clarity on your communication style:

1. Look at your last five text messages to your friends.

2. Look at your last five work emails.

3. Circle the words and phrases that appear in *both*. This is your core voice.

4. Do you sound like the same person? If not, which feels more "you"?

When I first started my coaching business, I hadn't yet found my authentic voice. And in marketing materials, it REALLY showed. I remember sitting down to write a newsletter to my email subscribers. While I don't have the exact email anymore, it went something like this:

Dear Valued Subscribers,

I hope this message finds you well. Today I wanted to address the important topic of work-life balance. Maintaining proper work-life balance is essential for professional success and personal well-being. Research shows that employees who prioritize self-care experience increased productivity and reduced stress levels.

Key strategies include:
Setting clear boundaries between work and personal time
Taking regular breaks throughout the day
Prioritizing adequate sleep and exercise
Scheduling time off to prevent burnout

Remember, taking care of yourself is an investment in your long-term success.

Best regards,

Kate

YAWN! Although I didn't use AI to craft that email (ChatGPT wasn't a thing yet), I read it back now and realize how boring I sounded. I was trying to be professional, but it lacked personality and fell flat. It should come as no surprise that I didn't get any replies, inquiries, or clients as a result of that email. It was generic and boring, and failed to show me in my best light.

If I were rewriting an email about work-life balance today, using my authentic voice, it would sound a bit different:

Hi y'all!

I just got back from an INCREDIBLE two-week vacation, and it reminded me why taking time off matters so much for your career success... and your sanity.

Walking through the bazaars of Istanbul and having tapas and sangria in Spain recharged my batteries, gave me a fresh perspective, and renewed my creativity – all things that benefit my clients and my business.

I know many of you struggle with actually using all of your vacation days. You might feel guilty about stepping away or leaving your team hanging. Last week, my client, Katie, told me, "Things are just so busy at my company right now. I can't imagine telling my boss I'm going on vacation at the time they need me most."

My advice? Take your damn PTO!!

Taking your (well-deserved) time off shows that you value yourself enough to sustain your contributions. The most successful women I know build in recovery and rest time. Your PTO days aren't a luxury. And they shouldn't be collecting dust... or even worse, being forfeited if you don't use them by a certain deadline. Taking time off is necessary for avoiding burnout and creating long-term career health.

Your next vacation might be exactly what you need to recharge your batteries (and get your sanity back). Trust me.

With a belly full of tapas and a heart full of love,

Kate

You can immediately see the difference between these two emails. The first email sounds like it could have been written by anyone (or any AI) about work-life balance. The second email could only have been written specifically by me, after my trip to Turkey and Spain.

Here are the key differences that make the second email authentically ME:

- I give personal details over generic advice.
- I tell real stories rather than discuss abstract concepts.
- It's my natural language vs. corporate speak (yep, I incorporated a cuss word).
- The tone is personality-driven, rather than distant and professional.
- The structure is more conversational than formal.

The first email is forgettable and replaceable. The second email is memorable, builds a connection, and is in my **authentic voice**.

If you use AI to communicate on your behalf, that authentic voice is lost. You aren't communicating as "you." You're communicating as the robot that is trained to impersonate you.

To further refine your authentic voice, here's a self-reflection exercise for you to complete:

Refining Your Authentic Voice	
Question:	**Your Answer:**
What topics make you light up when you talk about them?	
What words do you use that others don't? (industry terms, slang, or catchphrases)	
How do you naturally explain complex things? Do you tell stories? Give analogies? Guide someone step-by-step?	
What's your tone? Are you direct, humorous, warm, and analytical?	

Your answers to the questions above are part of your authentic communication style, which is uniquely yours. Your life experience and personality create a viewpoint and a communication style that only YOU can offer. The insights you have and the way you choose to express them contribute directly to your authentic success.

Reconnecting with Your Core Values

The things that are most important to you naturally influence your communication style. In Chapter 1, you identified your top two core values. If you don't remember what they are, go back to the Core Values Bracket exercise for a quick refresher. These core values drive your communication style. For example, someone who values accuracy will often think carefully before they speak, making sure their content is correct and delivered precisely. Or someone who values humor might make a point of being witty when they communicate, making others laugh, and making jokes to put people at ease.

Your core values make you who you are. ChatGPT can never replace or consistently emulate your ability to reflect them in writing. In fact, LLMs lack the concept of values entirely – they're <u>only</u> good at generating words. ChatGPT could never be you because an AI doesn't have **your** core values.

Authentic communication feels easier when it's aligned with your values. When thinking about my two emails from the previous pages, the first one felt forced, awkward, and just not "me." The second email felt almost effortless because it was authentically Kate.

Embracing Imperfection

I have some news for those of you who consider yourselves perfectionists: *Perfectly polished communication often feels inauthentic.* Consider politicians or highly rehearsed business magnates—does it feel authentic when they read something that was clearly written by a team of PR people? No! They sound authentic when a reporter catches them unexpectedly and gets a candid quote, because they had to speak in their actual voice, not their publicist's voice.

Think about the things that make you MOST nervous when you communicate with others—those minor imperfections, hesitations, and personal quirks that make you feel insecure. Is it that you talk too fast when you're excited or anxious? Or that you snort when you laugh? Do you get socially awkward in group settings? Maybe your cheeks turn red when you're self-conscious? These imperfections make you **relatable.** We are not perfect people, and we should embrace imperfection as a hallmark of humanity.

Being imperfect doesn't mean that your communication should be sloppy or riddled with errors. There's a difference between sloppiness and authentic human expression.

Sloppy Communication:	Authentic Human Expression:
• Typos and grammatical errors that distract from your message • Rambling without a purpose or direction • Using text speak in professional contexts ("u" instead of "you") • Sending messages when you're angry without taking time to think • Oversharing inappropriate personal details in professional settings	• Sharing a brief personal story that relates to your professional point • Admitting when you're wrong or don't know something • Using humor that reflects your personality (when appropriate) • Expressing genuine emotion: "I was disappointed by the outcome, but here's what we learned…" • Using your natural speech patterns and vocabulary • Adding brief context: "After my conversation with Sarah yesterday, I realized…"

Sloppy communication prioritizes speed over consideration for who you're talking to. It signals a lack of effort and makes it seem like you don't care about the person on the other end. Authentic human expression maintains clarity and respect while letting your personality shine through.

Let go of the pressure to sound like a corporate Communications Department. Have the courage to use your natural vocabulary and sentence structure, without relying on AI to write your emails or make them "better." Most importantly, understand that being imperfect is what makes you human and makes you relatable. Vulnerability in communication leads to **stronger** connections.

Brené Brown is a fantastic example of a powerful woman who communicates authentically. Brown is a research professor who has built a global leadership platform by using her authentic voice while maintaining her professionalism. She's consulted for Fortune 500 companies, speaks at major conferences, and has built a multimillion-dollar business. In her TED talks, books, and corporate consulting work, she doesn't sanitize her language or hide her personality to sound more "executive-like." She uses phrases like "Holy crap, this is hard" in professional presentations. She shares personal stories about her own struggles with vulnerability. Most importantly, she admits when she is wrong or uncertain.

Brown's authenticity doesn't make her less credible or professional. It makes her *more effective*. Her willingness to say, "I don't have all the answers," or, "This research scared the crap out of me," creates deeper trust and connection with her audience than self-certain, sanitized corporate-speak ever could.

She's genuine without being inappropriate, vulnerable without oversharing, and conversational without being unprofessional.

What can we learn from Brown? I encourage you to challenge the myth that professional communication must be sterile. There is a balance to be found between being polished and being genuine, and that's where your authentic voice lives.

Vulnerability as a Leadership Advantage

Showing your human side builds stronger relationships and better leadership skills. Research shows that vulnerability in leadership fosters trust, empathy, and growth. This inevitably creates a higher-performing team.

Being appropriately vulnerable makes you stronger as a leader, not weaker. When you admit mistakes or share struggles, people trust you more. This is especially important now because everyone's communication is starting to sound the same due to AI.

I once worked for a small business owner named Jennifer. She was great at being appropriately vulnerable at the right times. At one point, the company had a dip in revenue that was making cash flow super tight. Jennifer was forced to make decisions to tighten up company spending. She eliminated a few of our expensive software models, ended the relationship with an agency we'd been partnering with, and let go of a few employees.

When I initially heard the news, I was taken aback. I was scared about my own position and the company as a whole. Jennifer scheduled a meeting with the core team to communicate these decisions and explain the next steps. She showed up for that meeting, presenting herself as:

Vulnerable.

Authentic.

And honest.

Jennifer didn't hide her emotions. It was clear that these were difficult decisions for her. She wasn't sobbing on Zoom or anything, but we could see that it tore her up inside to be cutting back and laying people off. She was honest about the financial situation and the reasons that she needed to make these changes. She explained her next steps logically and went over her clear strategy for increasing revenue. She ended by thanking all of us for continuously being there and showing up to help her business succeed, even in the challenging times.

After hearing Jennifer speak from a place of such deep vulnerability and authenticity, I felt a stronger sense of trust, loyalty, and security within my place at the company. She was genuinely trying to make the best decisions for her business. She wasn't trying to ruin anyone's career or intentionally hurt anyone with her business decisions. After this meeting, I was even more committed to showing up and performing well in my role so we could get the company back on track.

As a leader, showing your human side builds stronger connections.

Here are some benefits of vulnerability for people in leadership positions:

- It improves team communication. Open and honest communication leads to more transparency, which leads to better problem-solving and collaboration.
- It strengthens relationships. When leaders open up, it creates an environment of mutual trust, where people are more comfortable sharing their own ideas and challenges. This fosters empathy and deeper relationships.
- It encourages authenticity and engagement. When leaders are genuine, they inspire team members to be more genuine.
- It boosts resilience. When you openly discuss setbacks or challenges, you model an adaptable, growth-oriented mindset. Seeing Jennifer get vulnerable and discuss how she was going to bounce back from the company's revenue issues, which inspired me to be resilient and bounce back as well.

Like all people, leaders have emotions, too. Hiding those emotions, or communicating in a way that is over-polished or too prepared, feels like a wall that keeps people out. Embrace authenticity and vulnerability. Allow people to see the real you—an authentic leader who isn't hiding her real self.

Leveraging AI without Losing Your Authentic Voice

It might sound like I've been talking a lot of smack about AI in this chapter. AI is incredibly useful when used as an amplifier, not a replacement, for your authentic voice. Let's talk about how to leverage AI to help you communicate more clearly and effectively—without losing your authenticity.

Think of AI as a microphone for your voice. It can amplify your message by making your writing more polished and your ideas easier to understand. You can prompt AI by providing your **original** thoughts and ideas, using AI to help you articulate them more clearly. Your personality and opinions should stay center stage, and you have full ownership over the ideas and direction. AI should NOT be your ventriloquist, putting words in your mouth. This happens when you ask AI to generate content for you, perhaps about topics you haven't completely thought through. AI creates the tone, perspective, and ideas for you. You become the "dummy," just moving your mouth to a ChatGPT script. Its output reflects the AI's training data... not *your* authentic ideas.

Consider the examples below:

AI as a Microphone:	**AI as a Ventriloquist:**
• You write, "I've been thinking about why our team keeps missing deadlines lately," and ask AI to help you structure it into a clearer email. • You share your personal experience with a challenge and ask AI to help you format it into a LinkedIn post. • You have strong opinions about optimizing a process at work and use AI to help you outline your argument more persuasively.	• You prompt AI, "Write a LinkedIn post about visionary leadership," without providing any of your own insights. • Having AI generate an apology without sharing what you actually want to say. • Using AI to create content about experiences you haven't had or opinions you haven't formed.

If you've ever copy-pasted directly from ChatGPT and used it as your own content, you're using AI as a ventriloquist. The words will fall into the uncanny valley, where people sense that something is "off" when they read it—that it doesn't sound genuine or like a human wrote it. This doesn't mean you shouldn't use AI at all, but use it as a *microphone, not a ventriloquist.*

You may find it useful to set some boundaries on where and how you use AI assistance. Are there any areas of your life you'd like to be "AI-free zones" where you want to remain 100 percent genuine and authentic, pledging not to use AI at all? Here are the areas of my life that I've dubbed my AI-free zones:

- Personal messages or emotional communications, like text messages to friends and family or one-to-one emails to my coaching clients
- Creative expression and artistic work
- First-person stories/anecdotes
- Messaging about my values and beliefs
- Relationship-building communications, like following up with people in my social circle or individuals I've met at networking events (personal touch really matters here)

In other areas of my life and work, I leverage AI—with clear conditions:

- **I use AI in some business communications**, such as creating meeting or session agendas based on priorities and objectives or polishing slide decks or resources I use with clients where I've developed the core content and strategy.
  - o Conditions: I need to be comfortable disclosing AI assistance to my clients, the ideas and content are entirely mine, and I review and revise extensively without directly copy-pasting.

- **I may have AI assist me on social media content**, such as brainstorming a list of potential topics that would make great social media posts or generating hashtags for an Instagram post I've already written myself.
  - o Conditions: The original thoughts and ideas must be mine, I edit the content to match my own voice (let's face it, AI doesn't have my killer sense of humor), I'm transparent about using AI when asked, and the content still reflects my own thoughts and opinions.

- **I use AI to facilitate outlining or structuring**, such as drafting an outline of my business standard operating procedures or creating an initial structure for a proposal where I have all the technical details.

In the areas above, AI has been useful in helping me be more efficient, productive, and thoughtful, while also maintaining my authentic voice. When it comes to the conditions to adopt when using AI, you should always be able to explain why you made each decision or defend every point in your final content, even if AI helped with initial drafts or outlines.

Now it's time for you to draft your Personal AI Policy. Fill out the worksheet below to determine your AI boundaries based on your values.

Part I: Your Core Values (refer back to Chapter 1 if needed)

List your top three to five core values:

1.

2.

3.

4.

5.

Part II: Values-Based AI Decision-Making

For each situation below, rate on a scale of 1-5 how comfortable you'd feel using AI (1 = never, 5 = always):

Personal Communication:
Writing a thank you note to a mentor: ____
Crafting an apology to a friend: ____
Writing a birthday message to a family member: ____
Drafting a sympathy card: ____

Professional Communication:
Writing a performance review: ____
Creating a client proposal: ____
Drafting internal team emails or Slack messages: ____
Developing marketing copy: ____
Writing your LinkedIn "About" section: ____

Creative Expression:
Writing social media captions: ____
Creating presentation content: ____
Drafting blog posts or articles: ____
Developing training materials: ____

Part III: Your Personal AI Policy

Based on your values and ratings above, complete these statements:
I will NEVER use AI for:

1.

2.
I will ONLY use AI for these tasks with conditions and/or transparency:

1.

2.

I'm comfortable using AI for these tasks without conditions or disclosure:

1.

2.

3.

Part IV: The Authenticity Test

Before using AI for any communication, ask yourself these three questions:

1. Would I be comfortable if the recipient knew AI helped with this? ____

2. Does this still sound like me after AI processing? ____

3. Am I using AI because I'm lazy or because it genuinely improves my message? ____

If you answered "no" to any of these questions, reconsider using AI for that task.

Review and update your Personal AI Policy Worksheet periodically. AI technology is constantly evolving, and your comfort level may also change.

Important Note: AI as an Accessibility Tool

While this chapter focuses on how to maintain your authentic voice, it's important to recognize that AI can be used as an accessibility tool for some populations. If you have dyslexia, ADHD, autism, or other cognitive disorders, using AI could help you with:

- Organizing your thoughts into a coherent structure
- Proofreading, spelling and grammar if those aren't your strong suits
- Translating complex ideas into clearer language
- Overcoming writer's block or communication anxiety
- Processing and responding to information more effectively

For all AI users, you still want to maintain your authentic voice and ideas while using AI to bridge communication gaps. The authenticity test still applies, even when using AI for accessibility. AI is here to help you express yourself more clearly, but your perspective and opinions remain YOURS.

Authentic Digital Presence

If having a strong digital presence is important to your career success, showing up authentically matters. This could be on LinkedIn, your business or personal social channels, networking or speaker bios, or anywhere else you have a digital footprint.

One of my favorite accounts to follow on Instagram is Rebecca Ives (@the_content_queen). Rebecca is a marketing expert who leads masterminds, sells marketing courses, and hosts a podcast. She has more than 35,000 followers and has made over $2 million from Instagram alone. I've followed Rebecca for years, and to me it's obvious how she has become a master at creating authentic digital content. It's because her content reflects her true personality and values. Rebecca has such a distinct, genuine, human personality that is reflected in all of her content. NO topics are off limits, and she fully embraces who she is, which makes her stand out from the crowd in an IG feed full of perfectly curated ChatGPT-generated captions and boring Canva templates. Here is one of Rebecca's recent Instagram captions:

Feminine Marketing Tip: Replace "networking" with business flirting

Once a week (ish!), when I'm feeling yummy, happy, full & in the mood to connect... I'll get on the internet and delight people in my network (friends, peers, past coaches & clients).

I'll leave deliciously thoughtful comments on posts. Engage in some witty DM banter. Offer unsolicited copy ideas. Connecting people to people who can help them achieve their goals.

There is zero agenda… other than making people smile/feel seen/get closer to their goals.

11/10 recommend

P.S. If a divine feminine marketing strategy that makes you millions is your jam? Stay tuned… something is coming.

The caption is paired with a video of Rebecca walking outside and blowing a kiss at the camera as a Selena Gomez song plays in the background. Her authenticity is refreshing. Reading her caption, you can probably pick up on her voice, personality, and values. She is feminine, supports and empowers other women, and values connection. She's not worried about being perfectly polished and well-liked; she's just worried about being her.

Here's what Rebecca shows me: Creating content that reflects your true personality and values is the number one way to have an authentic digital presence. Trying too hard to be "on brand" or fit into a certain box can make you sound disingenuous and even robotic. Let your genuine personality shine through! That's the juicy stuff people really connect with and really want to see.

Develop a style that is so distinct that AI *can't* replicate it. Use your core values to guide your communication style and show what you stand for. Share personal stories and experiences that only you can tell. Instead of focusing on putting some polished and beautiful (and frankly boring) version of yourself out there, aim to be authentically yourself.

What are the recurring themes that only you talk about? What is your distinctive way of approaching common topics in your life or your field of work? Start thinking through how these can serve as a framework to guide your digital presence—on social media, in email communications, and anywhere else you show up in the online space.

At the end of the day, AI simply misses the human touch. AI can't have a spontaneous reaction to current events or make jokes about corporate humor. AI can't reference your personal experiences, failures, or lessons learned. AI can't use your unique sense of humor. It tries, but there are often forced puns that are generic or don't quite land.

Instead of using AI to generate content, I challenge you to embrace your inner Rebecca and show up online as authentically as possible. Here are some things to try:

- Share raw, unfiltered thoughts (appropriately) and first drafts without heavy editing.
- Show behind-the-scenes content that shows your work process.
- Provide real-time reactions to relevant developments in the world or in your industry.
- Post content referencing recent personal anecdotes, experiences, or conversations.
- Ditch the heavy photo filters!

Building Trust and Authenticity in an AI-Driven World

As AI starts showing up <u>everywhere</u>, your ability to be authentic in your communication becomes your superpower.

There are certain types of communication where being human isn't optional. When someone needs an apology, is going through a tough time, or when you're trying to build real trust with them, AI just won't cut it. People can tell the difference. Remember, at the beginning of this chapter, the story about my friend who received an apology text that was written by ChatGPT? That's what we're trying to avoid. That text message broke trust and made a bad situation worse.

Here are some examples of situations where human touch is needed:

- *High-stakes emotional moments*: Apologies, conflicts, difficult conversations, delivering bad news, celebrating personal milestones, and crisis communication and support
- *Trust-building situations*: First impressions, new relationship-building, leadership during uncertainty or change, and mentoring or personal development conversations

It's tough because in some of these situations, your first thought might be, "I don't know what to say." It can be hard to find the right words to say to someone when you're having a difficult conversation or discussing a sensitive subject. That's why, during these times, it's even more important to communicate from within and use your own authentic voice. Communication is like a muscle. The more you use it, the stronger it gets. If you rely on AI to do the heavy lifting, that muscle weakens. When you consistently communicate authentically, even when it's uncomfortable, you build the strength to show up when it matters most

One of my former coaching clients, Kim, recently announced on social media that her father passed away. From our many coaching calls, I knew about her close relationship with her dad. I also knew about her dad's declining health. Immediately upon seeing Kim's post about her father's death, I wanted to send an email with my condolences. I found myself sitting at my desk, an email draft open, having no idea what to type. I admit, I pulled up ChatGPT and asked it to write an email expressing my condolences to my client who recently lost her father.

The email that ChatGPT spewed out sounded pretty and professional, but it was also totally lacking in compassion and love. I felt like using that version of the email was watering down the message and the true emotions I wanted to share with Kim. Frustrated with myself for even opening ChatGPT in the first place, I closed the tab immediately and started writing from the heart.

I wrote about how glad I was that Kim and her dad got to create their final memories together in the Colorado mountains, enjoying nature together. I wrote that her dad raised a great daughter, one who is ambitious, entrepreneurial, and vivacious. And I shared how much love I was sending her way from California.

An LLM could've never written that email for me. I don't know why I even thought to try. An email like that requires a personal touch. Being authentically human and spending the time to write that email is what made it meaningful when Kim received it.

Future-Proofing Your Authentic Success

As I'm writing this in 2025, everyone is freaking out about AI taking their jobs, particularly in the finance and tech industries.

This year alone, some major companies have cited AI as a reason for conducting layoffs. Microsoft laid off 4 percent of its total staff, indicating that AI tools are performing tasks previously handled by junior developers. Accenture laid off 11,000 people, citing AI adoption. Fiverr let go of 30 percent of employees as part of a strategic pivot to become an "AI-first company." Major tech companies are laying off workers and replacing them with AI to cut costs.

While we can't predict the future, the general consensus is that AI is taking over jobs that are:

- Based on repetitive, rule-based tasks
- Entry-level roles
- Data-driven professions
- Customer service and administrative positions

This rise in AI, while creating new opportunities, is also disrupting the job market and creating a TON of anxiety, especially for people early in their careers. The full impact of AI is still unfolding, but it's predicted that millions of workers will need to retrain in new fields or learn to work with AI tools to remain relevant in the future job market.

We've been here before. When computers first entered the workplace, people panicked. They thought machines would replace entire industries. Yes, computers did make certain roles more efficient and eliminated some positions. But they didn't *replace* humans– they changed how we work. AI is following a similar pattern. The tools are different, but the outcome will likely be similar: the humans who learn to work alongside the technology, not against it, will thrive.

There are authentic human skills that AI simply cannot replicate. Learning, honing, and becoming an expert at these skills are key to future-proofing your career.

Emotional Intelligence and Interpersonal Skills

ChatGPT can't show empathy or read someone's emotional state. Humans understand unspoken feelings, read body language, and respond to emotional needs in nuanced ways. Building genuine trust and rapport is what creates deep, lasting professional relationships based on mutual understanding. Only humans can navigate complex human dynamics, like managing office politics, resolving interpersonal conflicts, and building team culture. Sure, AI can analyze data and generate content, but it can't build that genuine human trust, read a room during a tense negotiation, or intuitively know when someone needs support versus a push. As more transactional work gets automated, the work that remains will be human-centered.

The companies that will succeed are the ones that realize that their most valuable assets (client relationships, team cohesion, and company culture) all rely on **authentic human connection**. If you can build and maintain those relationships, you'll be irreplaceable.

When it comes to high-stakes decisions and situations, people still want to work with humans whom they trust. Even if AI provides the data or the analysis, the final decision-maker who can weigh competing factors, read political dynamics, and inspire confidence will be a person.

Here are types of jobs where these skills will remain critical in the future:

- Client-facing roles: Account directors and customer relationship managers who maintain multimillion-dollar client partnerships, business development executives who build trust with external stakeholders, and customer success leaders who turn clients into long-term advocates
- People leadership and development: Executives who navigate complex organizational dynamics, HR leaders managing culture, conflict, and organizational change, and talent development professionals who groom future leaders
- High-stakes advisory: Management consultants solving complicated organizational challenges, executive coaches working

with C-suite leaders, and change management specialists
guiding companies through transformational periods
- Negotiations and partnerships: Sales leaders closing deals, business development professionals building strategic partnerships, and mediators and conflict resolution specialists

Creativity and Strategic Thinking

AI doesn't understand context the way a human does. You can draw on your lived experiences to come up with truly original ideas. AI can make decisions based on patterns it recognizes in the data, but only YOU can make decisions based on pattern recognition from real-life experiences. You might be thinking, "But AI is trained on so much human data. Can't it replicate our patterns?" You're right– AI is getting scarily good at mimicking human expression. But there's a difference between synthesizing millions of other people's experiences and drawing from your own. AI doesn't have lived experiences. It just has data points. It can tell you what someone might say in a situation, but it can't tell you what YOU would say based on the specific combination of your career, your relationships, your failures, and your intuition. That's yours alone. It's also no secret that AI sucks at cross-domain innovation. When it comes to connecting disparate ideas, humans are better at synthesizing in ways that algorithms can't predict.

Dr. Spencer Silver is an American chemist and inventor who co-created Post-it Notes, although it took a colleague's creativity to turn it into a marketable product. In 1968, Silver was trying to create a strong adhesive for the aerospace industry. He "failed" and instead created a weak adhesive that stuck to surfaces but didn't bond and could easily be removed. For years, this seemed like a pretty useless invention that didn't have real value in the commercial market.

A few years later, one of Dr. Silver's colleagues, Arthur Fry, was getting frustrated that bookmarks kept falling out of a church hymnal. During a church service, he realized he could use one of Dr. Silver's "failed" inventions to create bookmarks that would stick to the pages without damaging anything. Fry ran with the idea, developing the product and eventually earning the patents that brought it to market. This was the beginning of "Press 'n Peel" (Post-it Notes' original name), and it's still considered one of the most widely recognized product innovations in design history.

The creation of the commercial Post-it Note required authentic human skills and experience. Silver and Fry had to:

- Understand a failed chemistry experiment
- Recognize a mundane personal frustration
- Connect these two completely unrelated domains
- See potential where data would show "no market demand"

Could AI eventually make a connection like this? Maybe– if someone prompted it with exactly the right question. But no one was asking that question! There was no market research pointing to "sticky bookmarks" as a billion-dollar opportunity. It's more likely that AI would've categorized Dr. Silver's initial experiment as a failure against its intended purpose. It took a human sitting in a church pew, annoyed by a falling bookmark, to make the leap. AI is great at answering questions we know to ask. Humans are great at noticing problems we didn't know we had.

It was their *human experience* that created an innovation worth billions of dollars. You probably have some sitting on your desk right now, right?

This kind of cross-domain creative thinking—connecting a chemistry failure to a church hymnal problem to create a global office product—is authentically human.

Leadership and Influence

Who are people going to turn to in times when leadership is needed? They'll turn to a human with the ability to lead and influence—not a robot. These quintessentially human skills are things AI cannot replicate and will future-proof your career. Inspiring and motivating others to rally around a shared purpose is something only a human can do. AI might be able to make some black-and-white decisions and help you weigh pros and cons in certain scenarios, but a real human is needed for ethical decision-making in gray areas. There are situations where there's no clear "right answer," and a leader needs to make those nuanced decisions based on gut instincts and lived experience.

Then, there's leadership during times of crisis. When a company is going through something challenging, it's important for the leader to read the room and adjust their approach in real time, based on human needs.

Business problems are getting more complex as time goes by. Organizations are facing challenges that AI simply can't fix, like merging company cultures, leading through political ambiguity, and making ethical tradeoffs among stakeholder interests. These nuanced challenges need human judgment.

AI can optimize existing processes, but it can't create a compelling vision of the future that inspires people to change. Organizations need leaders who can articulate where a company is going and why it matters.

Here are the types of jobs where these leadership and influence skills will be critical in the future:

- Executive leadership: CEOs and C-suite executives who set strategic direction, VPs managing organizational transformations, and founders and entrepreneurs building companies
- Change management and transformation: Chief transformation officers leading digital or cultural shifts, change management consultants guiding organizations through restructuring, and innovation leaders creating new initiatives
- Crisis management: Any role navigating PR disasters or operational failures, turnaround executives brought in to save struggling organizations, and risk officers making judgment calls in crisis situations.

- Strategic partnership and alliance roles: Merger-and-acquisition leaders integrating acquired companies and strategic alliance managers balancing competing organizational interests
- Ethical and values-based leadership: Chief ethics officers navigating AI governance and responsible innovation, sustainability leaders balancing profit with environmental/social impact, and DEI (diversity, equity, and inclusion) roles creating inclusive cultures.

Working with AI Instead of Against It

One of the best ways you can future-proof your authentic success is to position yourself at the intersection of technology and humanity. If you can build skills that help organizations bridge the gap between human needs and AI, you'll become invaluable.

I've met many tech-savvy professionals who understand AI capabilities but struggle to apply them to human problems. Maybe they can't explain the technology in concise terms. They can talk to a computer all day but struggle talking to other humans. I've also met many professionals who are kind, persuasive, and charismatic but don't know how to leverage AI.

*The people who can do **both** will thrive in the job market of the future.*

Research shows that companies are investing billions in AI, but 85 percent of AI projects fail. Not because of bad technology, but because of poor human integration. If you can position yourself as someone who can help organizations adopt AI without alienating their workforce, you solve a BIG problem for them. Companies desperately need people who can implement AI, oversee change management, ask (and answer) ethics questions, and augment AI with professional services.

We're already starting to see high-value types of roles at this intersection:

- Chief AI ethics officers
- AI policy advisers
- AI transformation consultants

- Learning and development professionals training teams on AI collaboration
- UX (user experience) researchers studying how humans interact with AI systems
- Product managers building AI features
- Customer experience designers
- Lawyers using AI for research
- Doctors using AI for diagnostics
- Financial advisers leveraging AI analytics

Don't just rebrand yourself as "AI-fluent" without developing a real understanding and skillset. Companies need people who can bridge the gap, not just people who mention AI in their LinkedIn headlines. If you are genuinely passionate about both technological progress and human well-being AND you're willing to stay up-to-date with AI developments (it's advancing rapidly), this positioning might work for you.

Chapter 5 Recap:

1. Your authentic voice is your competitive advantage! AI can't replicate your lived experiences, personal stories, and genuine perspective.

2. Use AI as a microphone to amplify your ideas, not as a ventriloquist to create them. Maintain ownership of your thoughts and ensure outputs still sound like you.

3. Complete the Personal AI Policy worksheet to establish boundaries. Define your AI-free zones and areas where conditional use aligns with your values.

4. High-stakes emotional moments demand human touch. Apologies, difficult conversations, and trust-building require your authentic voice. People know the difference.

5. Embrace vulnerability and imperfection as leadership strengths. Your unique blend of experiences and personality is more powerful than AI-polished perfection.

6. Future-proof your career by developing irreplaceable human skills: emotional intelligence, creative thinking, ethical leadership, and strategic decision-making in ambiguous situations.

Connected Success:
How Relationships Fuel Your Authentic Journey

"One woman's success can only help another woman's success." – Gloria Vanderbilt, artist, writer, and pioneering fashion designer

The people you are closest to dramatically impact your life. You've probably heard the saying by Jim Rohn, "You are the average of the five people you spend the most time with." While you might not be *exactly* like your co-workers I believe this quote has some merit. I see it with my coaching clients all the time. Similar to your habits, the quality of your relationships also greatly influences the quality of your life.

My client Lindsey was a self-proclaimed "social butterfly" in her 30s living in Chicago. She worked in the HR Department of a prominent consulting firm and was one of those people who made friends everywhere she went. She would strike up conversations with people at coffee shops, fellow gym-goers, and those who also attended her many work events. As a result, Lindsey was well-connected and had strong personal and professional relationships both in her home base of Chicago and across the country.

When her company went through a reorganization and Lindsey's position was eliminated (along with thousands of others), she was devastated. She'd worked hard to grow the program she managed and had solid relationships with her colleagues and external partners. In our coaching, we quickly began working together to strategize and come up with a plan for her next career move.

It was clear to me that Lindsey's greatest asset in her job search was going to be her network. With so many connections made over the years, Lindsey had contacts she could immediately reach out to. As she began her outreach, Lindsey established allies in her job search. In these conversations, her contacts:

- Offered her practical advice and insights
- Sent her resume along to hiring managers
- Introduced her to new people they thought she would benefit from knowing
- Gave her access to the "hidden" job market by telling her about job openings at their company that weren't publicly listed on the company website or any online platforms
- Submitted internal referrals at their companies
- Offered her jobs on the spot when they discovered she was available – "If you want it, it's yours!"

Lindsey was blown away at how generous and helpful her network was. Within six weeks of being notified that her position was eliminated, she had a new job. This job came directly from one of her contacts in Chicago, who was a former coworker and recommended her for an open position. Lindsey was ecstatic to have landed not only a new job but also a job that aligned so well with her career goals and passions.

This is the power of relationships and networking in your life and career. I've seen it hundreds of times with my clients. Women with strong relationships and networks that they invest in regularly are more likely to feel supported, have new opportunities, and achieve their goals. You don't have to be a social butterfly like Lindsey to build and leverage your network, either.

Your connections expand your opportunities. A study on social networks conducted by researchers at Columbia University and the University of Wisconsin-Madison found that the average American knows about 600 people on a first-name basis. This means that if you're in a room with 20 people, you collectively know about 12,000 people. Those 20 people can link you to thousands of other connections! Each person you meet potentially connects you to hundreds more.

Having a strong network can fuel your success, unlike almost any other factor. It's much easier (and faster) to achieve your goals when you have allies working with you. Having strong connections:

- Opens doors to job opportunities (like Lindsey experienced)
- Provides you with resources, information, and insights you wouldn't have otherwise
- Creates a support system when you're dealing with tough stuff
- Gives you the chance to learn from others' experiences and expertise
- Increases your visibility in your community or your industry
- Builds your credibility or reputation by being associated with certain individuals
- Offers diverse perspectives that can improve your decision-making

A significant percentage of all new jobs are landed through networking. The research varies, but it's approximately 70-85 percent. Yes, your network matters that much for generating most great opportunities in your life. If you think about how you landed previous jobs, I would bet that several of them involved an introduction, referral, or recommendation. It's not luck, it's your network!

Debunking Myths About Networking

While I have some clients like Lindsey who network happily and naturally, the majority of my clients are more resistant. Some find it uncomfortable, some find it too time-consuming, and some would just rather be at home in their PJs watching "Bridgerton." It's easy to make excuses not to network. There are plenty of reasons to avoid it. However, I've found that many of the reasons people give for avoiding networking are based on myths or misconceptions. Let's debunk some common myths.

Myth #1: Networking is inauthentic or manipulative.

I remember the slimy real estate agent who handed me (well, shoved me) his business card in the middle of a casual dinner party with friends before even asking my name. I felt like I needed to wash my hands after that. Many professional women have told me they associate networking with being fake or transactional, rather than building genuine relationships. And I get that—it's people like that real estate agent that make us feel icky about networking. But the truth is that networking is just building relationships—something many women already excel at. *Authentic networking* means:

- Connecting with others on genuine shared interests or goals
- Listening more than you speak
- Offering to help someone without expecting anything in return
- Building a relationship before asking someone for something
- Finding a way to add value to others' lives and careers

Think about your strongest professional relationships. They probably didn't start out with a calculated approach to getting you something you wanted. They developed organically through common interests, mutual collaboration, and shared experiences. When you reframe networking as simply building relationships, you remove the "ick factor" and focus on making meaningful connections.

Myth #2: You need to be an extrovert to network effectively.

Many women I've coached think that in order to be a great networker, they need to be the life of the party—charismatic, working the room, and feeling energized from large events. If you're more introverted, this myth might keep you from networking because you feel like a fish out of water in a noisy room. But the truth is that introverts have a unique networking advantage. They often make *exceptional* networkers, but in a different way from extroverts. Introverts bring:

- Great listening skills, which allow others to feel seen and heard
- Thoughtful, meaningful conversations that lead to stronger relationships
- Quality connections over quantity

- Strong follow-up and one-on-one relationship maintenance
- Careful observational skills that help identify genuine opportunities to support others

Research by Susan Cain in *Quiet: The Power of Introverts in a World That Can't Stop Talking* shows that introverts often build more meaningful and lasting professional relationships because they focus on depth rather than breadth. If you're an introvert, don't try to be more extroverted! Instead, leverage your natural strengths. Some of the most successful networkers I've seen are introverts who play to their strengths, rather than trying to be more extroverted. It's not about how many hands you shake, it's about how many connections you nurture.

Myth #3: I don't have time for networking.

When life is busy, and you're juggling responsibilities at home and work, networking can feel like an extra task on your to-do list. Between family responsibilities, a demanding career, and attempting to maintain some semblance of self-care, the idea of adding networking to your plate might seem impossible. But networking doesn't have to be a separate activity that requires lengthy blocks of time, it can take more of an integrated approach. Remember my client, Lindsey, from the beginning of this chapter? Some of her strongest connections were made in the gym, by arriving to meetings a few minutes early to socialize, and even in the checkout line at Trader Joe's. She wasn't adding many additional events to her schedule. It started with her existing activities. Here are some simple ways to integrate networking into a busy schedule:

- Arrive 10 minutes early to a meeting to connect with colleagues
- Take an interest in the person sitting next to you at a conference you're already attending
- Follow up thoughtfully after interactions you're already having
- Reach out to a team member from another department on a current project

Another perspective is thinking about networking as a *time multiplier*. Building the right connections can provide shortcuts to information you'd spend hours researching on your own, connecting you with resources that can solve your problems more efficiently. It can also open doors to opportunities that align with your goals, so you can go further, faster. Networking doesn't require a huge time investment for it to be effective. Even 15 minutes weekly dedicated to building or maintaining your relationships is a good starting point that can yield bigger results over time.

Myth #4: Networking is slow and unpredictable with no guaranteed payoff.

"I attended an industry happy hour last night and met some cool people, but nothing came from it. There was no payoff!" I've heard this from clients who "try" networking but don't see immediate results, so they write it off. It seems like an unpredictable investment of time and energy with unclear results. In a world driven by quarterly goals and immediate gratification, networking can feel like an inefficient use of your time. The truth is that networking is a long-term game that's worth playing. You wouldn't ask someone to marry you on a first date, and you shouldn't meet someone at an industry event and immediately ask them for a job offer or major favor. Truths about networking as a long-term strategy:

- Building meaningful relationships takes time, consistency, and patience
- Genuine professional relationships built over time lead to trust
- People will go to great lengths for people they know, like, and trust
- Consistent, small touchpoints over time will create something meaningful
- There's a compounding effect in networking. Your returns don't just add up—they multiply!

While it's true that the payoff with networking isn't immediate, the compound interest from building authentic relationships makes networking one of the highest-ROI activities for your life and career success.

Myth #5: As a woman, I'm at a disadvantage when networking in male-dominated environments.

The Old Boys' Club. *Ugh*. Many women tell me that they avoid networking because they feel disadvantaged in industries or at events that are male-dominated. They feel that golf courses and sports bars are still the real centers of power and that they're an outsider looking in. Yes, even now, gender dynamics in networking are real. Some industries and settings remain predominantly male, and navigating these spaces can be uncomfortable or exclusionary. However, when you're one of just a few women in the room, you're naturally more memorable. Being different can be your greatest networking advantage. While this visibility can feel uncomfortable, it's a powerful differentiator in networking contexts where being remembered is half the battle. Instead of ignoring gender dynamics or avoiding male-dominated environments, I encourage you to navigate them strategically:

- Identify male allies who respect you and can open doors
- Seek out female mentors who have successfully built connections in your industry
- Bring your authentic perspective to conversations rather than trying to conform
- Be deliberate about creating networking opportunities for yourself
- Join women's professional groups in your field for additional support

And things are evolving! Many companies and networking organizations recognize that top talent can come from anywhere, and they actively seek out gender diversity in their networks, leadership, and events. What might have once been a disadvantage can now be an opportunity to connect with individuals who value diverse perspectives. While gender dynamics are a real thing, it's not an insurmountable challenge. The things that make networking feel difficult can also become unique advantages when you approach them with confidence and a strategic mindset.

Do any of these myths resonate with you? Is there one that you tell yourself as your own personal reason to avoid networking? In the box below, write which myth from above resonates most with you and why:

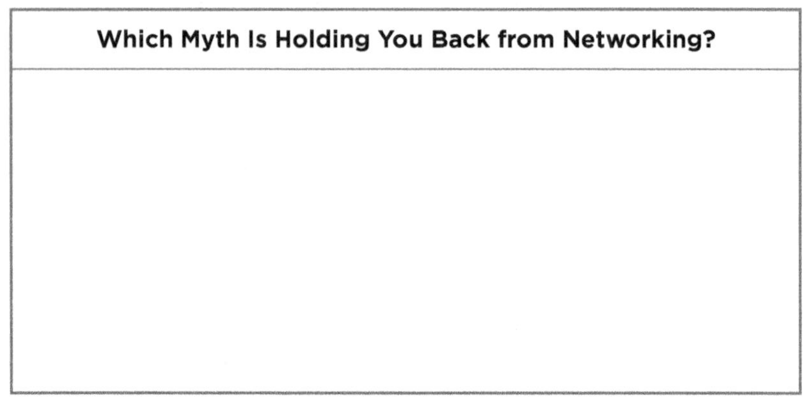

I encourage you to debunk that myth and start thinking of networking as a way to build authentic relationships. These relationships will support you, open up new opportunities, and ultimately enrich your life and your journey to authentic success.

Principles of Authentic Networking

Authentic networking is all about building relationships. When you're building real, genuine relationships, networking actually feels **good— not** scary, salesy, or uncomfortable.

For nearly five years, I was a member of a San Diego networking group of 20 local business owners across various industries. I had just started my coaching business and wanted to meet other entrepreneurs whom I could connect with, learn from, and eventually create a referral network with. When I first started attending this group's events, I was skeptical—for many of the reasons outlined above in our Myths About Networking section.

Our group met every Tuesday morning for a breakfast networking meeting. During the meeting, each member had an allotted amount of time to speak and introduce themself, give a brief overview of their business, and make a specific "ask" for the week. It could be a request for a specific referral, a Google review, or sharing information about an upcoming event. Then the featured presenter (it rotated each week) would have 10 minutes to give a more in-depth presentation on their business and help the group understand how we could support them.

After attending a few meetings, I felt more comfortable and started to see the value of this networking group. With members repeatedly introducing themselves and talking about their businesses week after week, the consistency started to create a feeling of familiarity. I gained a deeper understanding of what each business owner did, the services they provided, and how I could collaborate with them. It wasn't a "hit and run" networking event that I attended once and never saw these people again. It was the week-after-week connections that picked up right where they left off the week before.

From the beginning, the members of this group made a real effort to get to know me. They asked me lots of questions about myself and my business in conversations at the Tuesday meetings and in one-on-one meetups outside of the weekly group meeting. In one of my early meetings with the group's residential realtor, Bo, I was blown away at the thoughtful questions he asked me:

- "What specifically makes you different from other coaches?"
- "When I'm having a conversation with professional women in San Diego, what signs can I look out for that they might be a good fit to work with you?"
- "How can I support you and your business in being as successful as possible?"

When I answered Bo's questions and whenever I spoke in this group, I felt like I was truly listened to. They weren't just trying to sell me something or get referrals out of me—they were genuinely interested in getting to know me and forming a relationship. In return, I wanted to do the same! As a new business owner, I was curious to hear their insights and advice on starting a business, navigating the San Diego market, and learning from their successes. I was eager to ask questions and get to know them better.

I quickly realized that these networking partners were more than willing to send business my way. They inquired about my coaching services and wanted to know who my ideal client was. They stayed on the lookout for women they met in their day-to-day lives that might make good referrals for me. They asked me the best way to introduce their referrals to me. Within a few months, I was getting great referrals from this group. Our group's financial advisor, Alissa, sent an email introduction to her client, who was looking for help with salary negotiation. Bo referred his sister to me, who was just starting her own business. Our personal trainer, Till, shared my LinkedIn profile with his virtual client, who was looking for a new job, and she hired me almost immediately.

It meant a lot to me that my networking partners, who were beginning to feel like friends, were generous enough to send me business. And not just any business—these were their closest friends, family, and neighbors. Not only did it feel fulfilling and meaningful, but it also motivated me to want to do the same in return. I was excited to reciprocate and send my referrals to them. My cousin who needed new car insurance? I introduced him to our auto insurance representative. My friend who was starting a new chiropractic business? I introduced her to the group's CPA. The relationships I formed in this group were built on trust and personal connection, but they also became mutually beneficial to our businesses. In my first year after joining this group, my business made $10,000 in revenue directly due to referrals from my networking partners, a number that would only increase in subsequent years. New friends AND an extra $10k in my pocket? Yes, please!

My time in this networking group is a perfect example of authentic networking. Through this experience, as well as through coaching my clients through their own networking successes, I've developed five principles of authentic networking. These principles are the fundamental truths that will guide you to networking authentically.

Principle #1: Network in alignment with your values.
Your networking should reflect who you are and what's important to you. When your networking aligns with your values, it's more natural.

It also helps you connect with like-minded people who may approach life, business, or their careers in a similar way to you. For example, if *making a difference* is one of your core values, you may choose to focus your networking efforts on meeting professionals in the social impact space, B Corps, or nonprofits. You can attend events for causes you care about, join nonprofit boards, or get involved with a volunteer organization.

These types of networking situations clearly align with *making a difference*, and you'll meet other folks who share that same value. If you're volunteering for a cause you're passionate about, your authenticity and enthusiasm will shine through, making it easier to connect with others. Networking through volunteerism is a fantastic way to build a professional community in a more genuine environment than a "traditional" networking environment, like a happy hour at a dark, crowded bar. I've seen clients build strong relationships with people they've met through volunteering, which has led to mentorship, referrals, and job opportunities. Networking is a lot more comfortable (and fun) when it's aligned with your values.

Principle #2: Network for quality over quantity.

A few deep connections are more valuable than hundreds of superficial ones. Meaningful relationships require time and energy, but they often pay off in the long run. Focus on quality connections that are mutually beneficial. Let's say you're attending a conference. Your initial inclination might be to meet as many people as possible to maximize your time networking. But rather than trying to collect 100 business cards, set a goal to have five *truly meaningful* conversations. After the conference, follow up personally with those five individuals, referencing specific details from your conversation.

These five relationships will likely yield more value than dozens of forgotten contacts. How many times have you come home from a conference or networking event just to empty your purse of all the business cards you collected and throw them straight into the trash can? I admit, I'm guilty of this as well. If you focus on networking with the goal of building quality relationships instead of shaking as many hands as possible, your connections will be more valuable in the long run. You'll have authentic relationships with real people you've connected with over shared interests or goals.

Principle #3: Give before you receive.

Approach networking with a mindset of generosity. Focus on how you can help other people rather than what you can get out of networking. Offer help, information, or connections, without expecting immediate returns. When you give to others, it establishes trust—and reciprocity naturally follows. Just like my networking partners that started sending me referrals, I wanted to do the same for them.

Several years ago, at a networking event for Female Entrepreneurs of San Diego, I met a woman who was trying to break into real estate but didn't know how to get started. She'd been in property management for a decade but felt clueless about making a pivot to become a real estate agent. At the networking event, her goal was to meet people in the real estate world in San Diego. When we started chatting, I told her that—although I'm not a realtor—through my networking group, I knew several people in the industry and would be happy to introduce her.

Without expecting anything in return, I introduced her to two real estate professionals in my Tuesday networking group. For me, it was an easy introduction that didn't require much effort. I simply thought it could help this woman out with her industry pivot, and I had no idea where it would lead. It turns out, one of the people I introduced her to was a significant influence in this woman's pivot into real estate. He provided mentorship, introduced her to more people in the industry, and ultimately helped her land her next job. She was **beyond** grateful to me for the introduction. Since then, she has referred several of her friends and colleagues to me for career coaching.

This was unexpected! I didn't introduce her to my contacts with the thought that I would get anything in return. But by being a giver and hoping to add value, I ended up receiving business in return. When you meet someone new, ask yourself, "How can I help this person?" rather than, "What can I get from this person?" Can you introduce them to someone in your network that they would benefit from meeting? This generosity is often returned many times over.

Principle #4: Build long-term relationships instead of transactional interactions.

Authentic networking focuses on relationships, not transactions. Stay in touch with and nurture your connections, even when you don't need anything. Consistently reach out and touch base with your contacts and build a strong foundation for your relationship <u>before</u> you need something from them. For example, instead of only reaching out when you need a job referral (which can feel transactional), maintain regular contact. Share congratulations on their achievements, like a promotion or a new job, send them relevant industry news or events, and check in periodically just to see how they're doing. When you eventually do need their help, they'll probably be more responsive because you've built a real relationship.

Principle #5: Be genuinely interested in others.

Curiosity about others makes networking more natural and enjoyable. Ask thoughtful, open-ended questions and practice active listening. Remember the details about someone's life and follow up on them. Once, I mentioned to a networking partner how much I loved the taco scene in San Diego and that I enjoyed trying as many taco restaurants as possible in my free time. When a new taco spot in town opened up, she reached out and asked if I wanted to go there for a one-to-one meetup to discuss how we could help each other promote upcoming business events. I was touched that she remembered my love for tacos and took it into consideration for our meetup. I felt seen and heard, which fueled our connection (and YES, we did come up with some great strategies to promote each other's events).

These five principles will guide you to network authentically. When you align your networking with your values, prioritize quality over quantity, lead with generosity, build for the long term, and show genuine interest in others, networking transforms from a dreaded obligation into a natural extension of your professional self. The magic happens when you stop seeing networking as something you *have to do* and start having fun with it and seeing it as part of *who you are*. This shift makes networking more enjoyable, sustainable, and <u>effective</u>. It's all about allowing people to see the "real you" and creating opportunities that align with your authentic path to success.

Identifying Your Current Network

Your network is bigger than you think.

I asked my client, Linda, an employment lawyer in Nashville, "Do you have a warm network?" She immediately said, "No, not at all! I grew up in Texas, went to law school in Chicago, and my first job was in Georgia. I haven't been good about keeping up with people and I don't really know anyone in Nashville. My network isn't warm at all."

Having heard statements like this before, I smiled and continued to press Linda. I said, "OK, no problem. For the sake of identifying who you DO know, let's just start to brainstorm a list. No pressure for it to be a certain size. This list can be anyone you know from any part of your life. Start with the people you know well: your family, close friends, and neighbors. Then, think of people you went to undergrad or law school with. Write down former coworkers and bosses. Then get to casual acquaintances: your spin instructor, your best friend's husband, or the barista at your local coffee shop. Let's just start getting some names down on paper."

Linda started jotting down names and was **shocked** at how quickly her list grew. After just five or 10 minutes of brainstorming, she had a list of almost 50 people. Her list included:

- Friends and family
- Colleagues from previous companies/roles
- Current and past mentors
- Alumni from her university
- Connections from networking events (she was in several lawyers' clubs)

- Other attorneys she'd met over the years
- Family connections (like her parents' friends and relatives working in corporate)
- Neighbors in her apartment complex
- Acquaintances she met at the dog park
- LinkedIn connections

This exercise is simple, but for Linda it was a powerful reminder of how many people she actually knows. This is an important first step for anyone who wants to improve their networking skills or their relationships in general. **Start by identifying your current network.** Take inventory of all the people you know and notice how your list grows as you keep brainstorming.

Maintaining and Nurturing Relationships

Don't be a "hit and run" networker! You know those people who only reach out to you when they need a favor? That rubs people the wrong way! Invest in your network by following up and communicating regularly.

The networking group of small business owners I mentioned earlier in this chapter had one member, a website developer named Jon, who was exceptional at nurturing his relationships in our group. At least once monthly, I would receive an unexpected email from Jon. Sometimes these emails were news articles or recent studies that were relevant to my industry. Other times, he would forward me information about an upcoming event or webinar relevant to my coaching business. Beyond sending me emails, which were always personal to me or my industry, Jon was also consistent about planning times to meet up or have a Zoom check-in.

One time, Jon, his wife, and their adorable Dachshund puppy were hanging out at a local dive bar that happened to be two blocks away from my house. Knowing I lived in the neighborhood, Jon texted me earlier in the week and asked if I wanted to meet up with them for a beer. Sure enough, we met up at the dive bar and ended up getting to know each other better in a more casual setting—plus I got to make friends with his wife and pet their weenie dog puppy!

Other times, Jon would ask me to hop on Zoom for a 20- to 30-minute coffee chat just to check in and talk about business. During these Zoom chats, Jon would ask thoughtful questions like:

- "Do you have any upcoming business events or programs that I can help promote?"
- "What types of clients are you working with this week, and what are their greatest needs?"
- "Is there anyone in my network I can introduce you to?"

Jon was a master of maintaining and nurturing his relationships. The time he spent regularly investing in his network was incredible. Over time, I grew to really like Jon and trust him. He was consistent. He was reliable. And he was an excellent communicator. I felt confident that he took care of his customers with the utmost professionalism. After just a few months, I started sending people I knew who were building websites over to Jon. This required a high degree of trust, as Jon was often working with new business owners to design and launch their brand-new sites. In the years since I've known Jon, I've referred many of my friends and colleagues to him.

And it wasn't just me! Remember, our networking group had 20 members. I noticed at our weekly meetings that Jon had a steady stream of referrals coming from other members of our group. I believe it's because he took the time to invest in each and every one of us. It wasn't just me he was sending relevant emails to, chatting with on Zoom, and meeting for a beer. He consistently maintained his relationships with everyone in the group.

After knowing Jon for several years, I asked him, "Jon, how do you have time to network so often? I feel like you're always meeting up with other business owners, sending emails, and chatting with people in our group. How do you maintain that with all the clients you have?" He smiled as he responded,

"100 percent of my business is generated through referrals. Networking is the single greatest use of my time. Maintaining my connections is my top priority, so I schedule time for it—every day." That's right, **every day** Jon carved out two or three hours of his day strictly for networking activities. This could be meeting someone for lunch or coffee, scheduling a brief Zoom chat, attending a networking event, or sending "check-in" emails to people in his network. I'm not saying you should be networking for three hours of your workday, but I think we can learn an important lesson from Jon: *When you maintain and nurture your relationships, you create authentic connections with people who will support you, show you new opportunities, and go to great lengths to help you succeed.*

Here's what this might look like in your life:

- Schedule regular check-ins with key connections (a quarterly coffee meetup, a monthly email, etc.) and make sure to put it on your calendar
- Share relevant articles, podcasts, or opportunities without expecting anything in return
- Remember and acknowledge important milestones (promotions, work anniversaries, accomplishments)
- Create an Excel file or Google sheet to keep track of your connections and their interests/needs
- Follow them on social media and engage with their content
- Ask how you can support their current projects, events, or challenges
- Express genuine appreciation when someone in your network helps you

Don't wait until you desperately need a new job or really need a favor to reach out to your network. Be proactive and make efforts to stay in touch regularly and nurture each relationship. Someday, when you need it, those connections will be there for you.

Expanding Your Network

While nurturing your existing connections is important, there's tremendous power in growing your network. Your career is like a garden: you need to tend to what you've already planted while also introducing new plants and varieties to keep a diverse, thriving ecosystem.

Your current network is valuable, but it may have limitations. The people you already know and tend to spend the most time with may share similar backgrounds, perspectives, and sources of information. This creates a network that functions a bit like an echo chamber where similar ideas, opportunities, and insights circulate among the same people.

When you strategically start expanding your network, you'll get access to:

- **New perspectives:** People from different backgrounds or industries can see problems and opportunities differently than you do.
- **Diverse expertise:** Meeting specialists outside your immediate circle can provide new insights, wisdom, and ways of thinking.
- **Sources of inspiration**: Cross-pollination of ideas from different fields often sparks new inspiration and innovative solutions.
- **Unexpected allies:** People with complementary skills can help you achieve goals faster.
- **Hidden opportunities:** Many positions, projects, or opportunities are filled before they're ever open to the public.

My client, Rebecca, experienced this firsthand. She worked in nonprofit event planning for over a decade and had a strong network in the nonprofit world. Rebecca decided she wanted to change her career trajectory and was hoping to transition into corporate event management, but she didn't have strong connections in the corporate sector. She needed to strategically grow her network so she could meet people in corporate roles whom she could learn from and partner with to help her with her career transition.

Rebecca tried different approaches to expanding her network, like attending networking events, utilizing LinkedIn, asking friends for introductions, joining professional associations, and leveraging her university's alumni network. Although it took several months (remember, networking is a long-term strategy), Rebecca expanded her connections to include contacts at large corporations and hospitality groups, many of whom worked in corporate event planning and management. Eventually, it was one of these new contacts who referred Rebecca to an open role at her company that she ultimately accepted, successfully making her transition into corporate.

If Rebecca had only networked with her connections in the nonprofit world, she wouldn't have landed her new corporate job. Being strategic about expanding her network and meeting new people is the reason she was able to make this transition! So how *exactly* did she do it? Let's get into the nitty-gritty details of it.

WHO, WHERE, and HOW to Grow Your Network

Expanding your network isn't about collecting business cards or sending random LinkedIn connection requests. It's about thoughtfully broadening your circle in a way that authentically aligns with your goals.

Start by identifying **WHO** you want to meet:

- What *industries or roles* are you targeting?
- What *perspectives* are missing from your current circle?
- What *knowledge areas* would benefit from your career?
- Who has *wisdom or influence* in an area you want to grow?

Once you're clear on WHO you want to meet, decide WHERE you're going to meet them. **WHERE** do these contacts spend time?

Professional Associations or Industry Organizations

These groups exist specifically to help facilitate networking and new connections. Look beyond the obvious organizations in your field and explore groups that align with where you want to go in the future, even if it's an industry where you don't have experience (yet).

Volunteering and Board Service

Offering your skills to causes you care about not only makes a difference but also connects you with like-minded individuals across various industries. Serving on nonprofit boards or committees can give you the opportunity to meet community leaders or executives you wouldn't meet otherwise. One of my clients, Keely, served as a board member in Chicago for a nonprofit that provided youth leadership training to underserved communities. She was in charge of fundraising and individually raised quite a bit of capital for the organization. When a fellow board member heard that Keely was job hunting, they were excited to tell her about an opportunity at their company (a Big 4 accounting firm). That relationship that Keely built through her board service resulted in a new job at KPMG that she wouldn't have otherwise landed—or even known about.

Alumni Networks

Your university offers a built-in network of people who share a common experience. Your fellow alumni are predisposed to help fellow graduates, making these connections easier than completely cold outreach. Oftentimes, there are virtual ways to connect with your alumni network—through a university website platform, social media groups, or even university-specific job boards. If you went to a large university, many US cities will have informal alumni groups that host events or reunions. When I first moved to San Diego, I was pleased to find a San Diego Aggies alumni group that helped me meet other Texas A&M alumni and build relationships with people I connect with regularly.

LinkedIn

LinkedIn is so much more than an online resume. It's a platform that offers powerful opportunities to expand your network strategically. On LinkedIn, you can connect with professionals all over the world while also showcasing your own skills and expertise through thoughtful content and engagement. You can search for contacts by industry, company, job title, and other filters. You can get extremely specific about who you target, so you're not just sending random connection requests. Don't just collect connections—engage meaningfully through direct messages, commenting, and joining relevant groups. LinkedIn has the power to connect you with people you might never get the chance to meet in person.

Conferences and Events

Industry-specific gatherings provide concentrated opportunities to meet tons of new connections in a short period of time. Once again, this isn't just about collecting business cards. It's about finding more focused or intimate opportunities, like breakfast roundtables, evening receptions, and smaller workshop groups, to develop authentic connections. I met one of my strongest networking partners (and now closest friends) at a coaching conference in Dallas five years ago. We sat next to each other during one of the sessions and ended up having lunch together with a small group. Because we specialized in different areas of coaching (her in mental health, me in career), we shared mutual curiosity and interest in each other's business. Plus, we just happened to get along really well.

Based on that strong initial connection and some intentional follow-up after the conference, we remained in touch, despite living on different coasts. We regularly refer new clients to each other since our coaching specialty areas don't overlap. If it weren't for attending that conference, I would've missed out on a boatload of referrals—and a wonderful friend.

Learning Environments

Courses, workshops, and certification programs put you in a room with other people who share your interest in professional development or business growth. These shared learning experiences naturally build connections. While attending a continuing education event to keep her Project Management Professional (PMP) certification current, my client, Charlotte, ran into several former colleagues whom she hadn't seen in years but had been meaning to get in touch with as she explored new career opportunities. Seeing them at the PMP event gave her the perfect opportunity to reconnect and arrange times for one-on-one follow-up conversations.

Although the above networking opportunities are more organized events, groups, or platforms, you really can expand your network **at any time.** You never know when a casual conversation could lead to a learning experience, job opportunity, or great friendship.

Now let's talk about the **HOW.** How do you approach these networking situations authentically, with genuine curiosity and value to offer? Here's how:

- **Do your homework.** Before you reach out to someone individually, learn about a person's work, background, experience, interests, and recent accomplishments. This research makes sure you're prepared when you reach out, starting a conversation that is personalized and thoughtful, rather than generic.
- **Find common ground**. Look for points of connection. This could be shared interests, mutual contacts, complementary work experience, or aligned values. Finding common ground creates a natural bridge for conversation.
- **Lead with value.** Whenever meeting someone new, ask yourself, "How could I help this person?" Rather than focusing on what you could get from them, think of how you could provide value. This could be sharing a relevant article, offering a specific insight, or making an introduction to someone in your network.
- **Be clear and concise.** No one likes having their ear talked off. Respect people's time by communicating in a way that clearly expresses why you're reaching out and what you'd like to discuss. If you schedule a one-hour meeting, show you respect their time (and your own time) by ending promptly at the end of the hour.

- **Prepare your elevator pitch.** This should be a brief, authentic introduction that shares not just who you are, but what you do and why it matters.

Following Up Effectively

The magic of networking happens in the follow-up. All of the new people you meet won't help you if you don't follow up with them. Let's be real—most business cards end up in the trash, and then people wonder why the networking "didn't work." It's because there was no follow-up! The difference between a quick interaction and a valuable network connection comes down to follow-up.

Once I started to grasp the importance of **follow-up** in networking, I made some changes to my networking approach. The results were incredible. I used to go to networking events to meet people, socialize, have a drink, and cross my fingers that maybe one person would send me a client someday. When I realized how important following up was, I started taking it more seriously.

Here's how I shifted my networking approach:

- I started sending personalized LinkedIn connection requests within 24 hours of meeting someone new.
- I referenced specific details from our conversation in my follow-up message to show I was genuinely engaged.
- I tracked all new connections in a simple spreadsheet, so no one fell through the cracks.
- I always suggested a clear next step, like a coffee meeting or virtual chat.
- I set calendar reminders to check in periodically with new connections.
- When appropriate, I made introductions between new connections and existing contacts.
- I followed them on LinkedIn or other social media platforms and engaged with their content.

- I prioritized quality follow-up with a few promising connections rather than a generic outreach to everyone.

The results were pretty remarkable. The people I met at networking events became more than just business cards. They became partners, clients, and friends. They became supporters of my business. They referred their sisters, friends, wives, and colleagues to me. The difference wasn't how I was showing up at the event. The difference was how I was nurturing the relationship afterward. It was ALL in the follow-up.

When you follow up with people you meet at networking events, networking becomes less transactional and more about relationship-building. If you want your networking contacts to become valuable new connections that contribute to your success, following up and remaining in consistent communication is a nonnegotiable.

Chapter 6 Recap:

1. Your connections dramatically expand your opportunities. Research shows that 70-85 percent of jobs are landed through networking, not through formal applications.

2. Authentic networking is about building **genuine relationships**, not collecting business cards or making transactional requests.

3. The most effective networking follows five key principles:

    - Aligning with your values
    - Prioritizing quality over quantity
    - Giving before receiving
    - Building long-term relationships
    - Showing genuine interest in others.

4. Your network is likely much larger than you realize! Take inventory of all your connections from different areas of your life to see the true scope of your existing network.

5. The magic of networking happens in the follow-up. Consistent communication and relationship maintenance transform casual contacts into valuable connections.

Learning and Leading: The Reciprocal Journey of Mentorship

"A mentor is someone who sees more talent and ability within you than you see in yourself and helps bring it out of you." – Bob Proctor, self-help author, speaker, and success coach

When I think about the most significant influences in my career, I don't think about books, courses, or even my college degree. I think about **people**—the mentors who saw something in me that I couldn't see in myself yet.

Throughout history, mentorship has been a powerful force for personal and professional growth. Socrates mentored Plato, who mentored Aristotle. Ruth Bader Ginsburg mentored her clerk, Goodwin Liu, who is now a state Supreme Court justice. These relationships pass down wisdom and shape the thinking of leaders, who then influence the future.

Studies have shown the powerful impact of mentorship:

- **People with mentors are happier at work.** A 2019 CNBC/SurveyMonkey poll found that 91% of workers in mentorship programs are happy in their jobs.
- **Women with mentors experience accelerated professional growth.** According to a Catalyst study, women with mentors

are 50 percent more likely to be promoted and 25 percent more likely to hold senior leadership roles.

- **Mentorship increases your confidence and empowers you.** A Women Ahead study found 87 percent of mentors and mentees feel empowered by their mentoring relationships and have developed greater confidence.

Despite the proven impact of mentorship, it's surprisingly underutilized, especially by women in their careers. In fact, a 2019 study by Olivet Nazarene University found that 76 percent of people think mentors are important, but only 37 percent of people currently have one. That number should be much higher! Part of the gap might be availability. Great mentors aren't always easy to find. However, I think many women don't actively seek mentorship because they don't want to "bother" someone or they feel like they should be able to figure it out on their own. I believe *everyone* needs a mentor—someone to help you grow, learn, and elevate your skills and career as a whole.

Let's clarify what mentorship actually means, because it's often misunderstood.

Mentorship is a relationship where a more experienced person (the mentor) provides support, guidance, and wisdom to someone with less experience (the mentee) to promote their growth and development.

But it's way more than advice-giving! Effective mentorship involves:

- **Mutual respect** and **trust**: These are built on confidentiality and genuine care for each other's well-being.
- **Growth**: The primary focus is on developing the mentee long-term, not just solving immediate problems.
- **Two-way learning**: Wisdom may be primarily passed on from mentor to mentee, but both parties should learn and grow from the relationship.
- A balance of **support** and **challenge**: Effective mentors compassionately push their mentees beyond their comfort zones.
- **Authenticity** allows both people to be genuine and honest, rather than performing or posturing.

What mentorship is NOT is equally as important to understand. **Mentorship is NOT:**

- A manager-employee relationship (though managers can sometimes be mentors)
- One-way instruction or teaching
- A quick fix for career challenges
- Therapy
- Networking with an agenda

The greatest mentors I've ever had were a husband-wife entrepreneur duo named Steve and Susie Baskin. In their early years of dating, Steve was attending Harvard Business School and Susie was studying healthcare administration at Northwestern's Kellogg School of Management. They got married, moved to New York City, and Steve began his career as an investment banker at Goldman Sachs. Two years in, the couple decided that the frenzied, money-hungry NYC life wasn't for them. They decided to move to rural Texas to start a sleepaway camp for kids, a dream Steve had since he attended summer camp as a kid. One camp became two, two camps became three, and next thing you know, Steve and Susie were involved in summer camps across the country. And these weren't dinky little mom-and-pop summer camps. These were profitable, award-winning, elite summer camps—places where tech executives, professional athletes, and celebrities sent their children.

In my early 20s, Steve and Susie hired me as a director at Camp Champions in Marble Falls, Texas. While a job at a summer camp is quite different from a job in the corporate sector, I learned some of my most valuable leadership skills working at that camp. This was largely due to the fantastic mentorship I had from Steve and Susie.

Steve would charge me with developing new ideas and leading innovative and experimental projects. One such project was leading a new partnership that Camp Champions was forming with a youth development organization in Beijing, China. The concept of summer camp was brand new to China in 2014, but there were several organizations (with deep pockets) that were interested in the benefits of American summer camp for Chinese children. Steve named me as the liaison between Camp Champions and the Chinese Camp Association. My role was to develop a program that would recruit 30+ campers and three counselors from China each summer to attend our summer camp. This was totally uncharted territory for me! I had never been to China, nor did I speak Chinese, and knowing very little about the country, I was unsure where to start.

But Steve believed in me.

He introduced me to his contacts in China who could help facilitate the program development, and I was off to the races. I was petrified the first time Steve told me he was flying me to China to meet with our colleagues in person and meet with Chinese campers and their families. In the days leading up to the trip, he helped me develop a plan to build relationships with our Chinese stakeholders and make the most of my time there. Steve was well aware that this trip was pushing me outside my comfort zone, but he trusted that I would rise to the occasion and get the job done.

And he was right.

My first trip to Beijing was a huge success! Not only did I build strong relationships with our partners there, but I also represented the camp well at family recruitment events. We had a number of new camper enrollments, as well as new hires to join our staff the following summer. I also had the opportunity to speak with Chinese families about their hopes, expectations, and goals in sending their children to summer camp.

I went to China three more times after that to represent Camp Champions. On my last visit, I presented at the China Camp Association's annual conference to a room of 200 Chinese youth development professionals on the cultural benefits of American summer camp for Chinese children.

None of this would've been possible without Steve's mentorship. He provided me with guidance, support, and wisdom to help me gain leadership skills, develop my public speaking abilities, and grow in my cross-cultural competency. He trusted and respected me, knowing I would represent the camp well abroad. He kindly pushed me to grow, knowing I would stretch myself to new levels.

Susie was an equally fantastic mentor. Often referred to as the "camp mom" by our camp families and staff members alike, Susie is one of the most gracious and compassionate women I've ever met. What really sticks out to me about Susie's mentorship style was her ability to help me learn from mistakes and fail forward.

Yes, I made mistakes during my time working at the camp. One time, I gave a prospective camp family incorrect pricing information. Another time, I mishandled a camper situation, and we got a nasty phone call from a parent. And then there was the time I promised a staff member that we could make an accommodation that just wasn't possible. I made mistakes that were not OK, and Susie was the mentor I turned to in these tricky situations. I never felt judged, shamed, or scolded by Susie. She was extremely solution-focused, and she went beyond just helping me solve the immediate problem. She also helped me figure out how I could avoid making the same mistake in the future. Were there certain processes or systems I needed to follow or change? Were there different communication approaches I needed to try? Were there new things I needed to learn to be a more effective leader?

Susie genuinely cared about the growth of the camp, as well as my own growth as a professional and as a leader. Like Steve, she supported me as well as challenged me. She knew I was capable of more, and she helped me learn from my failures so I could be better.

Susie and Steve's mentorship has been a powerful force in my authentic success journey. They helped me:

- Develop my confidence in uncharted territory
- Learn to embrace calculated risks
- Build my resilience through failure
- Discover leadership skills I didn't know I had
- Learn to represent my values authentically on a global stage

I still often think about the lessons I learned from Steve and Susie. What I learned from them is applicable to my current situation as a coach, leader, and small business owner. I also coach my clients on similar concepts that they instilled in me. The mentorship that they provided to a young woman in her 20s is still rippling out over a decade later, making a difference on a larger scale.

Becoming a Mentee

Sometimes you get lucky, and your boss happens to be a fantastic mentor, taking you under their wing and giving you the support and guidance you need to grow in your career. But this isn't always the case. Think about a boss you've had that was NOT a great leader, much less someone you would want to call your mentor—we've all had one. When that happens, you need to be proactive and seek out potential mentors yourself.

The best place to look for a mentor is usually within your current organization. There are likely more seasoned employees who understand the company culture and politics and can give you guidance on internal advancement, and they might even have direct influence on your career progression.

Here's where you might find potential mentors at your current company:

- Senior leaders in your department or adjacent departments
- People who have made career moves or transitions that interest you
- High performers two or three levels above you (not just your direct supervisor)
- Cross-functional partners who excel in areas you want to develop

It might be tricky to find these people initially if you don't already have regular interactions with them. That's where you have to be strategic about <u>visibility</u>. Put yourself in situations where connecting with them is more likely. Volunteer for cross-functional projects or tasks that bring together people from different departments in the company. This gives you a natural reason to work alongside new people who could turn into potential mentors. Attend company-wide meetings, events, town halls, or training sessions where senior leaders are present. Make a point to ask thoughtful questions or speak up during discussions.

If you work at a company that has Employee Resource Groups (ERGs), formal mentorship programs, or lunch-and-learn sessions, show up and take advantage of them! These opportunities are goldmines for meeting people outside your typical circle. Visibility is being intentional about putting yourself in rooms where these potential mentors are (whether in person or virtual) and being brave enough to start the conversation (more on this to come).

Avoid mentors who might create conflicts of interest in performance reviews or promotions. A former coaching client, Sarah, mentored someone on her team whom she directly supervised. Her mentee would often come to her and share things like frustration that she didn't get promoted the previous year, criticism of the company's way of handling a situation, and even the fact that she was considering looking for new jobs.

When annual reviews came around, Sarah had a tough time evaluating her mentee objectively because of what had been shared in private conversations. While she didn't hold her mentee's comments against her, she was put in an awkward situation and struggled to separate their mentoring relationship from her evaluation responsibilities. A better approach would be for this mentee to find a mentor *she can be completely open with about her goals and challenges without creating complications.*

You can also look outside your current company to find potential mentors. Some other places you can look:

- **Professional associations or industry groups:** This could be the alumni group from your college/university, industry conferences or professional development events, or professional societies relevant to your work (for example, Accounting & Financial Women's Alliance).
- **Organizations and extracurriculars:** You might meet potential mentors while volunteering or participating in community service, serving on a nonprofit board, participating in professional development or certification programs, or attending an event hosted by a speaker or author you admire.

- **Digital events and social media:** LinkedIn is one of the most valuable spaces for networking in our virtual age. You can also participate in online communities or forums, connect with thought leaders whose content resonates with your goals, or attend virtual events.

- **Unexpected places:** Mentors can sometimes show up where you least expect them. It could be a customer or client who demonstrates leadership qualities, vendors or partners that work with your company, parents of your friends who work in your industry, or other local business leaders you meet while out in the community. I kid you not, I found a mentor at a coffee shop one time. We struck up a conversation while sipping lattes at tables next to each other, and it turned out she was a career coach who had been in business for almost two decades. We talked nonstop for the next 30 minutes as we finished our coffees, exchanged contact information, and made plans to meet again for coffee the following week.

From that chance meeting through today, she continues to give me incredible wisdom and insights from her expert perspective and experience. When we first met, I was a brand-new "baby coach" and was looking for all the help I could get. She generously shared her journey with me, gave me advice for what she'd do differently if she could start all over, and introduced me to a few other coaches in her network. She's still someone I view as a mentor and get together with regularly.

Now that you know **where** to look for potential mentors, let's discuss what to look for. You can't just assume that someone who looks successful or has a fancy job title is going to be a great mentor. It's deeper than that.

There are some qualities that come to mind right away when I think about a great mentor:

- They've achieved success in skills or fields you're targeting in your career. You want someone who already has *great results* in the area in which you want to grow.

- They have a learning mindset. Remember, mentorship involves two-way learning. You want someone who is still growing and evolving, not resting on past achievements.
- They have a good reputation and integrity. If others speak highly of them and respect their character, that's a good sign.
- Their communication skills are strong. You want a mentor who can articulate their thoughts clearly and give you constructive feedback.

Beyond these professional qualities, "soft skills" matter, too. A great mentor is likely someone who is patient and empathetic, honest and direct, and has high emotional intelligence. There's also a lot to be said about the personal connection and rapport you have with someone who is going to mentor you. The best mentors will see potential in you *that you might not even see in yourself* and help you develop it authentically.

Think back to my mentor, Steve. He saw my potential to be an international liaison, recruiter, and speaker long before I realized my own capabilities. He was direct with me about what I needed to do to set myself up for success and gave me regular feedback. He knew that I would rise to the occasion and helped me authentically develop the skills, mindset, and actions to make it come to fruition.

Here are some red flags—signs that someone won't be a great mentor for you:

- They only talk about themselves. Ugh, we all know someone like this.
- They give generic advice or surface-level suggestions. If they're telling you tips you could find on Google or LinkedIn, they might not understand your specific situation.
- They're unavailable or unreliable. If they take forever to respond to your emails, cancel on you, or just don't seem to value your time, move on.
- They push their own agenda. I've seen mentors try to make "mini-me" versions of themselves rather than helping their mentee become their **own best self**.

At the end of the day, you need to trust your intuition when it comes to approaching someone about mentorship. Someone can have the right credentials, experience, and reputation on paper, but the most successful relationships are built on mutual respect and genuine connection. Pay attention to how they make you feel when you're talking to them. Are you feeling inspired, seen, energized, and empowered? Or do you feel like they're just going through the motions or lecturing you? If someone makes you feel seen and heard, challenged in a supportive way, and inspired to grow, those are good signs that they could be an effective mentor for you. But if something feels off, like their communication style, their availability, or simply a personality mismatch, trust your gut and look for someone else.

The best mentoring relationships feel natural and energizing for both parties, not forced or one-sided.

Asking Someone to Be Your Mentor

Once you've identified someone you'd like to be your mentor, the next step is reaching out. And while this can feel intimidating, most people genuinely want to help. Many will be flattered that you thought to reach out to them. People like feeling valued for their experience and expertise. They like knowing that they're making a difference in someone else's career. So when you reach out, remember that you're not bothering them—you're giving them an opportunity to do something meaningful.

Start with a direct but informal ask. You can reach out via email, LinkedIn, or your company's messaging platform (Slack, Teams, etc.) with a message like this:

Hi [name], I saw your presentation on [topic] and was really impressed by your approach to [specific thing]. I'm working on developing my skills in this area and would like to learn from your experience. Do you have 20 minutes for a coffee or a quick chat?

This message shows that you've paid attention to their work, explains the reason for reaching out, and makes a small, specific request.

You're not asking them to commit to being your mentor forever—you're just asking for one conversation.

If that first meeting goes well, follow up afterward with a message along these lines:

Thank you so much for taking the time to chat with me. Your insights on [specific topic] were incredibly helpful. I'd love to continue learning from you if you're open to it. Would you be willing to meet quarterly (or monthly) to discuss my professional development?

This gives them an easy out if they're not interested or don't have the time. It also makes it clear what you're hoping for. Honestly, most people will say yes! You've already shown them that you're thoughtful, prepared, and genuinely interested in learning from them.

Making the Most of Mentorship

In the initial meeting with your mentor, make sure to talk through your expectations. What you're trying to achieve should be clear to both parties. Agree on the duration and frequency of your meetings. I typically suggest meeting with your mentor once a month, but it could be more often if you have an important project or career decision coming up. Ask your mentor about their preferred method of communication and meetings. Will you meet in person and grab coffee? Will you meet over Zoom? Can you call or email them regularly? You might also want to discuss the duration of the mentorship relationship. In some situations, it makes sense to agree upon a six-month or one-year period, or it could be ongoing. The important thing is that you open up the conversation about expectations early on to avoid confusion down the road.

You'll also want to talk about boundaries with your mentor. What topics are fair game, and what topics are off-limits? Your relationship might be career-focused, skill-specific, or broader life guidance. It depends on what you're looking to get out of the mentorship. Your mentor is someone you know on a professional level, but you might develop elements of friendship. That is GREAT, but you also want to respect boundaries and not be overly casual with your mentor.

Several years ago, I was mentoring a woman we'll call Yvette. I was not Yvette's direct supervisor, but we worked on adjacent teams, and she was hoping to grow in several of the career areas I was already excelling in. She asked me if we could start meeting monthly for conversations focused on helping her grow professionally. After a few months of productive and energizing in-person meetings together, Yvette brought up to me that she was romantically interested in a friend of mine, a man who used to work on my team at the company but had recently left to pursue another professional opportunity.

At first, Yvette's questions were totally innocuous. She'd been single for a long time and asked a harmless question about his relationship status, which I answered. But then, she brought him up again in another meeting. And then again. *And again.*

I found myself questioning what Yvette actually wanted to get out of our meetings. I remember asking myself, "Does she really want to work with me to improve her leadership skills? Or is she just using our time together to get a date with my friend?"

When I finally confronted Yvette with my questions about her intentions, she was embarrassed. While yes, she was romantically interested in my friend, that wasn't her purpose for meeting with me. She told me that she thought we were bonding as women and that discussing him seemed like a common interest. Once I straight-up told her that it wasn't something I was interested in discussing, we got back on track with her initial goals and kept it more professional. Looking back, I wish I had more clearly discussed expectations and boundaries from our very first meeting. It would've made that conversation a lot easier (and less awkward).

My meetings with Yvette continued until she left the company a year later, and her growth in that time was incredible! But the point here is: Have the discussion early about professional boundaries vs. personal friendship elements.

Just like anything else in life, *what you put into mentorship is what you'll get out of it.*

This should go without saying, but come prepared for your meetings with your mentor! Have specific questions to ask them rather than vague requests for advice or wisdom. Share updates on progress you've made since you last saw them and recent wins or accomplishments. Have a few clear challenges you're working to overcome and the context around them. And, most importantly, have clear goals in place for what you want to accomplish or discuss in each meeting. Your mentor will appreciate your structure and organization, and it will make it easier for them to give you their most targeted, personalized insights based on your unique goals and challenges.

Be an active listener. Take notes during conversations so you can refer back to them and follow through on actions they suggest. This makes it easier for you to implement them and report back on outcomes or lessons learned. If your mentor gives you advice that's unclear or doesn't resonate, ask clarifying questions.

After each business trip I took to China, I would sit down with Steve, and we would have a debrief meeting. In these meetings, we would catch up on how my trip to China went and what it meant for the camp, but it was also a time for mentorship and development. Beyond business outcomes, I shared what specifically I did well, like cross-cultural communication or public speaking. I also shared the challenges, like overcoming financial objections and trying to get potential staff members to understand our needs and priorities. Not only would we develop an action plan for next steps with our Chinese colleagues, but Steve would also give me specific suggestions, feedback, and next steps for my own professional development. Going into these conversations prepared with talking points helped me get the most out of Steve's mentorship.

Common Mentorship Mistakes (and How to Avoid Them)

As far as I know, no one gives you a *How to Be a Mentee* book in high school or college. So becoming a mentee can feel a bit like trial and error. There's not just one way for mentorship to work; personality dynamics and communication styles can really impact the relationship. In my coaching business and in my career, there are a few mistakes I've seen mentees make that have cost them really great mentors.

1. **Treating your mentor like a therapist.** I've seen mentees use their mentorship session to vent about workplace drama, personal problems, or emotional issues without looking for actual mentorship. Don't come to a meeting with your mentor looking to vent. It's not your mentor's job to be your therapist. While it's OK to bring up challenges and express frustration (you're not a robot, after all), be careful that you don't confuse emotional support with professional development. Be solution-oriented, and your mentor can help you with strategies to better handle whatever got you so frustrated. Don't just complain the whole time. Find a therapist or counselor for personal emotional support. And if you just need to bitch about your crappy day, do it with your girlfriends at happy hour, not with your mentor.

2. **Being passive.** Don't just show up and expect your mentor to drive the entire conversation and give you their magical insights. Remember, what you put into this is what you'll get out of it. Your mentor's skills won't rub off on you by just being in their presence and breathing the same air. Have specific questions ready to ask your mentor, bring updates on previous advice, and be ready to actively engage in problem-solving, rather than just sitting and listening.

3. **Seeking approval instead of guidance.** As a recovering people-pleaser, this one hits home for me. This is when you want your mentor to validate decisions you've already made, rather than truly seeking their guidance or input. Even if it's tough, you'll get more out of mentorship if you release the tendency to seek approval and reassurance rather than honest feedback. I used to do this all the time—I just wanted my mentor to be proud of me! They often were, but was that really helping me grow? Not really. Be open to having your assumptions challenged. And if you're uncertain about a decision, ask questions.

4. **Letting your ego run the show.** Do you ever get defensive when you don't agree with feedback or constructive criticism you've been given? That's your ego talking. You'll be amazed at how quickly you can grow when you allow yourself to open up to advice, even (especially!) if it feels uncomfortable. Listen to your mentor fully before responding, and fight the urge to argue or dismiss advice that isn't positive. It's OK to ask clarifying questions if you're uncertain about their criticism, but try to accept their feedback objectively, even if it stings your pride a bit.

These mistakes can be avoided if you have consistent ongoing communication with your mentor, clear expectations and boundaries, and regular check-ins about how the relationship is working for everyone involved.

Giving Back: Becoming a Mentor

Be willing to help someone else on their authentic success journey. Mentoring another person and watching them succeed is one of the most gratifying feelings in the world. It's one of the reasons I became a coach! But you don't need to have the title of "coach" or even be in a formal leadership position to be a mentor. All it takes is a willingness to develop someone else professionally, care for and respect them, pass along your wisdom, support and challenge them, and show up authentically and honestly.

Becoming a mentor is more than just a rewarding feeling. Research shows that it also **enhances your own success**. I've seen it firsthand—you become a stronger leader and ultimately more successful when you give back and mentor someone.

Why does becoming a mentor make you *more* successful?

- It forces you to articulate your knowledge clearly in a way that someone else understands
- It keeps you current and challenged
- Your network expands
- Your leadership and communication skills continue to develop

- You create a reputation for being someone who invests in others
- It gives you fresh market intelligence
- You reinforce your own learning

Of course, the purpose of mentoring isn't for your own personal gain; it's clear that there are many benefits of becoming a mentor.

Most importantly, becoming a mentor gives you the chance to give back in a way that could be really meaningful for someone else in their career journey. Mentors can have a huge influence on someone's career, possibly being even more impactful than a college degree.

Let's take some time to reflect on your personal views about mentorship. Write your answers to the questions about mentorship below:

Question:	Your Answer:
Who is the mentor you would've wanted early on in your career?	
What kind of influence would have been a game-changer for you?	
What feedback helped you get to where you are now?	
Who gave you that piece of wisdom that made everything come into focus?	
Who believed in you and pushed you to be better?	

Be that person for someone else. They might learn things from you that they would never learn on their own... and this could entirely change the trajectory of their career.

How to Be a Great Mentor

The best mentors are fantastic listeners. As the old saying goes, "We have two ears and one mouth, so we can listen twice as much as we speak." As a mentor, this is especially true. Instead of blabbing advice at and talking *at* your mentee, be an active listener and listen to understand, not to respond. Reflect back to them what you're hearing to ensure you understand, pick up on any unspoken concerns or emotions, and create space for your mentee to process their thoughts.

Asking open-ended questions is my favorite way to get people talking. Asking "yes/no" questions is really limiting and doesn't promote self-discovery or deeper thinking. Use "what if..." scenarios to explore possibilities and help them think through consequences before making decisions. Asking questions that challenge assumptions and encourage self-growth (without being confrontational) is a great way to get your mentee to find their own answers, rather than telling them what to do. There's a fine line between offering direct advice and helping them figure it out themselves. Try to balance wisdom-sharing with skill-building.

Part of being a great mentor is giving constructive feedback. The mentorship relationship should feel like a safe space where you can have a difficult conversation and share that feedback, even if it's tough. When giving feedback, your timing and delivery matters. In these conversations, make sure to:

- Use specific examples (not just general observations)
- Discuss behaviors and outcomes, rather than personality traits
- Recognize their strengths
- Identify clear areas for improvement

When it comes to giving feedback, modeling and teaching your mentee a growth mindset will help them see challenges as learning opportunities. Some folks struggle with feeling like any setback or challenge they encounter makes them a failure. If you can help them frame these setbacks as new information and learning lessons, you'll encourage that growth mindset. And when they make progress or have an accomplishment to share, celebrate that progress and effort. Their wins are your wins!

Consider the constructive feedback conversation below. Maria was one of my clients, and I've recreated this conversation based on what she told me during a coaching session because I think it highlights great mentorship on her part. Maria started noticing that her mentee, David, a mid-level marketing manager, had been struggling with dominating conversations during team meetings. Maria, a director, addressed this after hearing feedback from David's team.

Maria: David, I want to talk with you about something I've observed in your team meetings. I've noticed you tend to jump in with solutions pretty quickly when your team brings up a challenge. What are you thinking when that happens?

David: I guess I want to be helpful. When I see a problem, I usually know how to fix it, so why waste time?

Maria: That makes sense. Your instinct to solve problems is one of your strengths. How do you think it impacts your team members when you provide the solution right away?

David: Hmm... I hadn't really thought about it. I guess they don't get to work through it themselves.

Maria: Exactly. I've actually heard from a couple of your team members that they sometimes feel like their ideas aren't heard or valued. They want to contribute more, but they're not getting the opportunity.

David: I didn't know that they felt that way. That's definitely not what I want.

Maria: I know it's not intentional. Here's what I've learned about leading teams: Sometimes our job is to resist the urge to be the smartest person in the room. What do you think might happen if you asked more questions before offering solutions right away?

David: They'd probably take more ownership of the solutions. And they might come up with ideas I hadn't thought of.

Maria: Exactly. You might try counting to five after someone presents a problem, then asking something like, "What potential solutions have you considered?" or "What would success look like here?" Your role shifts from problem-solver to problem-solving facilitator.

David: That's actually harder than just giving the answer.

Maria: True, but that's what separates good managers from great leaders. Are you willing to try this in your next few meetings, and then let's talk about how it goes?

David: Yes, I can do that. Should I say something to my team about changing my approach?

Maria: What do you think would be most effective?

David: Maybe I could just start doing it differently and see if they notice? Or, actually, I could probably acknowledge that I've been jumping to solutions too quickly and ask for their patience as I work on being a better listener.

Maria: I like that second approach. It shows self-awareness and invites them to be part of your growth process. Let's check in next week about how it goes.

YES, MARIA! This is such a spectacular example of giving a mentee actionable, constructive feedback. Here's why Maria's approach works:

- She starts with a specific observation, not judgment
- She asks David open-ended questions to help him figure it out himself
- She validates his strengths before getting critical
- She suggests a specific strategy he can implement
- She ends with commitment and follow-up

Another aspect of being a great mentor is creating career development opportunities for your mentee, when possible. You might not be able to offer them a job, but how can you open strategic doors that will help them grow in their career? This might be making thoughtful introductions that benefit both parties, so your mentor can grow their network. It could be recommending your mentee for stretch assignments or projects that will help them showcase their skills and increase their visibility. Or you could invite them to meetings or events where they can learn and network.

The most effective mentors remember that their role is to develop independent, confident professionals, not dependent followers.

The Ripple Effect of Mentorship

Your mentorship actually makes a big difference on a larger scale. There are literally hundreds of studies showing the benefit of female mentorship. Consider these stats:

- According to research by the Anita Borg Institute, in the tech industry, 77 percent of women with mentors are more likely to stay in the industry after three years, compared to those without mentors.
- Women who have a mentor often feel increased loyalty to their employer. A 2022 Carson Group study on women in financial services showed that 61 percent agreed or strongly agreed that a mentor improved their work performance.
- Women mentors contribute to a safer and more respectful workplace culture. A Pew Research Center poll found that a significantly higher percentage of adults see female executives as better at creating safe and respectful workplaces than male executives.

Beyond impacting the individuals you mentor, you're making a bigger difference for women in the professional world. You're improving retention of female talent at your organization, increasing loyalty and work performance, and even creating a healthier, more respectful work culture.

Mentorship is bigger than just helping one person. You're increasing female representation in leadership and fostering career advancement for women as a whole. Isn't that what shattering the glass ceiling is all about?

Chapter 7 Recap:

1. Mentorship is a developmental relationship built on mutual respect, trust, and two-way learning. The most effective mentors provide both support and challenge.

2. Look beyond credentials to find the right mentor. Focus on traits like genuine interest in others' growth, strong communication skills, and emotional intelligence. Trust your intuition and seek mentors who make you feel heard and inspired to grow.

3. Being a great mentee means coming prepared with specific questions, actively listening to feedback, and following through on commitments. Avoid treating your mentor like a therapist. Embrace constructive criticism as a pathway to growth.

4. Becoming a mentor enhances your own success! You'll develop your leadership skills, expand your network, and build your reputation as someone who invests in others. The best mentors listen more than they speak, ask thoughtful questions, and focus on developing independent, confident professionals.

5. Mentorship creates a ripple effect that extends far beyond individual relationships. Women who mentor other women contribute to increased retention, improved workplace culture, and greater female representation in leadership, ultimately benefiting entire organizations and industries.

Sometimes the best mentors aren't the ones in your day-to-day work life. Mentors at your company are valuable, but they can only see you through the lens of your current role and environment. Having a mentor who brings an outside perspective is powerful. Someone who asks hard questions, challenges your assumptions, and helps you see possibilities you can't see from the inside.

That's often why women hire me as their career coach. They want a trusted advisor focused on their success. A mentor who is there during the most critical moments of their career. I've had the privilege of being that person for hundreds of women, helping them get unstuck, step into bigger roles, and expand their influence. If that kind of support sounds like what you need right now, scan the QR code below to learn more about working together.

Authentic Through Adversity: Staying True to Yourself When Life Gets Hard

"The most beautiful people I've known are those who have known trials, have known struggles, have known loss, and have found their way out of the depths." – Elisabeth Kübler-Ross, Swiss-American psychiatrist

It started with pain in my feet that took me from being a marathon runner to a couch potato. One day, I woke up, and the knuckles in my fingers were the size of cherry tomatoes. Then fatigue took over my body, and I found myself not being able to get through a full workday. I wasn't myself, and I knew something was "off" but wasn't sure what.

I was finally diagnosed with rheumatoid arthritis (RA) at 33 years old, after over two years of awful pain and seeing seven different doctors. RA is a chronic autoimmune disease that attacks the body's immune system and causes inflammation in joints, organs, and organ systems. The cause is unknown, and there is no cure, although there are ways to manage symptoms.

The diagnosis was devastating. Although I was happy to get answers about what the hell was happening in my body, knowing that I had an incurable condition that I would likely have to deal with for the rest of my life was a huge mental challenge. Not to mention the pain that just wouldn't go away. Anyone who has dealt with chronic pain knows not just the physical toll it takes on your body but also the mental toll it takes on your psyche.

I was running my business, coaching nearly 20 women, planning a wedding, *and* I was desperately trying to improve my health. I felt like everything was crumbling on top of me. Have you ever felt like that? Like you're drowning in your own life and can barely keep your head above water?

I remember thinking, "I coach amazing women every day on confidence, leadership, and career development. How am I supposed to be a great coach to them when I feel like a disaster in my own life?" I was angry. I was sad. I was exhausted. *And I felt weak.*

I did NOT feel like the strong, empowered, sunshine-happy "Kate" that I wanted the rest of the world to see.

I did not feel authentic, and I certainly didn't feel successful.

Sometimes life gives you challenges that just don't feel fair. We all face them at some point. You might also be struggling with an illness, injury, or health condition. You might be going through a breakup or divorce. You might be up to your eyeballs in credit card debt. You might be grieving the death of a loved one, or maybe you were just laid off. Whatever big challenge you're dealing with, it probably feels like it's derailing you completely.

Is it possible to still be and feel authentically successful when you're navigating life's darkest moments? I wish the answer was as simple as "Yes, of course!" But the answer is a bit more complicated than that.

In this chapter, I'll discuss the lessons I've learned about authentic success in times of adversity—both through my own experience with RA, as well as through coaching clients during their most challenging moments.

Give Yourself Grace

One of the most frustrating parts of RA was (and still is) that I'm not physically capable of doing the things I could before. I can't run more than two miles without my feet flaring up, whereas a five-mile run used to be my daily morning routine. I now require at least eight hours of sleep nightly to prevent fatigue, when I used to be able to run on five hours of sleep. I need at least 30 minutes of buffer time in between work calls or meetings to give myself plenty of time to take care of my physical needs and restore my energy, when I used to schedule back-to-back calls for six hours straight with no problem.

When I was first diagnosed, I held myself to the same standard I held pre-RA. As a lifelong high achiever (I'm sure many of you can relate), that was my standard operating mode. Of course, I was going to run five miles every morning. Of course, I was going to push through a tiring day even if I didn't get enough sleep. Of course, I was going to squeeze as many client calls as possible into one day without taking breaks—because I'm a machine!

And when my body was incapable of doing those things? **I felt like a big fat failure.**

Navigating RA meant learning to give myself grace. I practiced being kind, understanding, and forgiving when I wasn't meeting and exceeding the ridiculously high expectations I put on myself. One of the things that helped me the most with feeling true to myself was acknowledging my limitations and treating myself with the same compassion I would offer a close friend.

Instead of beating myself up for not running or exercising every morning, I told myself, "Kate, you're taking care of yourself and doing what you need to do to heal. Not running doesn't mean you're lazy or weak. There are other ways to be strong that don't involve running or physical exercise." At first, I didn't believe those words when I said them out loud to myself. But after a few weeks of consistently saying them, I started to believe them. After repeating those words to myself, the same way I would say them lovingly to a friend, it started to sink in. I began to believe that I didn't always need to push, push, push. I could give myself some grace and cut myself some slack.

Giving yourself grace often means changing your expectations of yourself. In Chapter 4, we talked about the habits of authentic success. These habits are the day-to-day actions that get you closer to reaching the big goals you set for yourself. When adversity strikes, those daily habits may not be realistic anymore. Whatever challenge you're facing may necessitate a change in what you're able to accomplish in a day. Some habits might need to be tweaked, and others might need to be dropped altogether. I had to drop running altogether—it just wasn't feasible for me. But did that mean I was incapable of exercising altogether? No! It took some trial and error, but I realized I could swim without pain, do yoga, and walk on soft, grassy surfaces. Instead of forcing myself to run through the horrendous pain in my feet or sit on the couch feeling like a failure, I developed new healthy exercise habits of swimming laps at a nearby gym a few times a week and doing yoga on weekends.

This habit change was a huge way of showing myself grace. Although technically I was "doing less" (running fewer miles, working out for fewer minutes, burning fewer calories—whatever I thought "less" meant), I found new ways to move my body that still honored my fitness values and wouldn't cause me pain. These new exercise habits were small ways for me to stay in alignment with my own vision of authentic success.

When you face a big challenge in your life, you'll likely need to change your habits, too. You simply won't have the same time, energy level, emotional capacity, or drive. Tweaks will need to be made—and that's OK! Give yourself permission to adapt your normal success habits and make changes that will better serve you during difficult times.

Here are some examples of what giving yourself grace might look like:

- Taking longer to respond to emails without over-apologizing: "Thanks for your patience as I work through some personal matters."
- Declining social invitations when grieving without feeling like a bad friend
- Ordering takeout for dinner during a particularly stressful week instead of cooking from scratch
- Saying no to nonessential work projects during a divorce or major life transition

- Delegating more tasks during a health crisis instead of trying to do everything yourself

Giving yourself grace is crucial for maintaining your well-being during these tough times. Acknowledge your struggles without criticizing yourself and create the space you need for staying true to yourself and healing emotionally.

Practice Gratitude and Recognize Your Wins

When going through difficult times, it's easy for us to fixate on what's going **wrong**. When I first got diagnosed with RA, I constantly said things like, "I didn't get enough work done today," "My body just doesn't work like it used to," and "I'll never feel like my old self again."

Looking back on those thoughts still makes me feel a deep sadness for what my past self was going through. I allowed negativity and self-criticism to take over my mind, and I saw the world through a very negative lens. I was so focused on what was going wrong that I couldn't see that there were still a lot of great things happening in my life. While this sadness and grief is a very normal part of being diagnosed with a chronic condition, I was fixated on what was going wrong and the negativity consumed my mind.

I've seen this with friends and clients before, too. My client, Elaine, had been unemployed for six months and was extremely frustrated with her job search. During our coaching sessions, she would say things like, "Nobody wants to hire me," "I should be doing more networking, but I just don't want to," and "I'm never going to find a job." Elaine's frustration took over and made it difficult for her to see the light at the end of the job search tunnel. Instead, she was focused on how terrible things were at that moment.

Have you ever been there? Life gets hard, and you just focus on the bad things, forgetting to zoom out and see the bigger picture or remember the positive. You say things like:

- "I *should have* done that, but I didn't have time."
- "I *could have* done this better, but I was exhausted."
- "I *would have* worked harder, but I had other things on my mind."

Sound familiar? Let's talk about how to leave the *shoulda-coulda-woulda* behind, especially when you're facing something really difficult. That thinking only leads to more negative feelings like guilt, anxiety, frustration, anger, worry, sadness, or defeat.

In his article, *The Grateful Brain*, neuroscientist Dr. Alex Korb discusses the idea that you can't be anxious and grateful at the same time. This is because your brain physically cannot respond to both positive and negative stimuli simultaneously. When you're feeling stressed, anxious, or worried, **gratitude is a solution**.

Practicing gratitude doesn't come easy when you're going through something challenging. I sure as hell didn't feel grateful for my body (or anything else for that matter) when the RA pain was consuming me. And I'm sure my client, Elaine, didn't feel grateful for the roof over her head when she was panicking about getting a job. The reality is that practicing gratitude is a proven way to flip your brain into positive thinking and away from negativity, even if it feels forced at first.

There is *always* something to be grateful for, even when you're going through difficulties.

Through my RA journey, I made the intentional choice to look for things to be grateful for. And yes, I had to force myself to do it at first. I ordered a gratitude journal from Amazon and literally made myself sit down for five minutes at the end of the day and write down things I was grateful for. Here are some things that made my gratitude list consistently:

- My husband for taking care of me and cooking meals when I was low-energy
- A great rheumatologist whom I trusted with my care plan
- The financial means to pay for the medication I needed
- Supportive friends and family who would check in with me and tell me that they loved me
- A beautiful sunrise or sunset

When I shift my attention to these things I'm grateful for (and even as I type this now), I immediately feel uplifting emotions: love, positivity, and warmth. It might sound cheesy, but the truth is that **gratitude is an antidote to stress.**

There's no wrong way to practice gratitude. You don't need to buy the Amazon gratitude journal like I did. But the crap that you're going through now will almost certainly feel more manageable when you incorporate gratitude into your daily life.

Other suggestions for practicing gratitude:

- Write a thank-you letter to someone you appreciate. You don't even have to send the letter, and you'll still get the brain benefit from going through the process of writing it.
- Make gratitude part of family life and share what you're grateful for during mealtime or before bedtime.
- Keep a gratitude bowl. Write one thing you're grateful for on a small piece of paper and put it in a small bowl that you keep somewhere visible in your house, like a coffee table or kitchen counter. Every time you walk past it or see the bowl, envision what's written on the paper and feel your gratitude.
- Say "thank you" for the little things your loved ones do that you normally take for granted. When your spouse takes out the trash or picks up groceries, say thank you. When your sister offers to watch your kids, say thank you.

Pick a gratitude practice that is realistic and sustainable on a daily basis. It doesn't need to be complex or time-consuming. The best gratitude practice is the one that you can stick with consistently.

Beyond practicing gratitude, it's so important to recognize yourself for your wins. These can be the things in your life (big or small) that are positive, areas of progress, or things to celebrate. I've found that many people, especially high-achieving women, often focus on the negative, criticize themselves, harp on what they could've done better, or ruminate on the past. This is especially true when you're facing adversity in your life.

In every coaching session, I start by asking my clients, "What are you proud of yourself for this week?" It's a simple question, but it helps break the habit of self-criticism. By adopting a new habit of recognizing your wins and being proud of yourself, you shift away from the *shoulda-coulda-woulda* and instead feel positivity and progress.

I've heard responses like:

- "I've been rolling with the punches. That's usually hard for me, but lately I've been flexible, and it feels really good!"
- "I pulled off a huge event with less than 90 days of preparation time and it went SO well! I got my team involved, delegated effectively, and asked for help."
- "I landed three new clients, woohoo!"
- "I've been sticking with my exercise and working out consistently. It feels so good to be back in a routine with moving my body."
- "I confronted my coworker about a tough situation, even though it was nerve-wracking. I stood up for myself and held a boundary."

Let's kickstart your new practice of celebrating yourself. What are you proud of yourself for this week? Write it in the box below:

This Week, I'm Proud of Myself for...

By getting in the habit of acknowledging why you're proud of yourself, you're rewiring your brain to focus on your strengths, accomplishments, and growth. This practice builds confidence, resilience, and a positive self-image over time.

When Elaine, my client from earlier in this chapter, was struggling with her job search, I would consistently ask her what was going well or what she was proud of herself for. She would tell me things like:

- "I applied for three jobs this week."
- "I went to a networking event and connected with the owner of a marketing agency who wants to schedule a time for us to chat."
- "I've been going to spin class every morning."
- "I have a preliminary interview with an exciting company."

By sharing her wins and recognizing her progress with me weekly, Elaine started to internalize that, even though she was frustrated with her job search, she could truly see momentum, progress, and many reasons to feel excited about the future. When Elaine finally did land a job, she found that continuing her gratitude practice and celebrating her progress kept her mood up and made her a stronger leader.

Recognizing your wins, no matter how small they are, is important for maintaining your well-being during challenging times. Acknowledge your progress and feel proud of yourself! This allows you to stay true to yourself through a more positive lens.

Draw Boundaries and Say 'No'

Setting clear boundaries is always important, but it's even more essential when you're going through something challenging. When shit hits the fan, you simply might not have the time, energy, resources, or emotional capacity that you used to when things were going swimmingly. Making adjustments is necessary. Saying "no" is necessary.

I've always been a social butterfly who loves spending free time with my friends. My mom told me that when I was 4 years old, I would go out on the front porch of our house and yell, "Friends, where are you?! Who wants to come over and play?" I hoped that the neighbors' children would hear me and want to come socialize. This social mentality continued through adulthood, and I kept a very busy social schedule with my various friend groups. It was fun!

But when the RA hit…
I was fatigued.
I was in pain.
I was exhausted.

Getting enough rest became more important than socializing.

I had to start drawing boundaries and saying "no" to friends and social invitations. It was the only way to stay well-rested and continue healing every day. Waking up early to play beach volleyball with friends? No, I needed to sleep in and have a slow morning. Going to a concert downtown with a group of friends? Nope, that would kill my energy. Having a long beach day with friends? Nah, I need my nap and my heating pad nearby. Going to a friend's house to watch movies and drink wine on a Friday night? Well, maybe I kept doing that one, but only if I was back home and in bed by 10 p.m.

Why is saying "no" so difficult? So many of the women I coach struggle to draw boundaries and say no to others. I can't speak for everyone, but in my case, it definitely stems from people-pleasing. According to *Psychology Today,* people-pleasers "need to please others for reasons that may include fear of rejection, insecurities, and the need to be well-liked." Many of us (myself included) struggle with saying no because we fear we will upset the other person, causing them to not like us as much. I also worried that people would stop inviting me to do things because they thought I would always say no. It was all my own insecurities. But the reality is that saying no typically doesn't cause severe social consequences.

Saying no became much easier when I realized that saying no to something meant saying yes to something else.

When I declined social invitations, here's what I was saying yes to instead:

- Sufficient sleep
- Time to relax, recharge, and restore my energy
- Self-care: taking a long bath, stretching, meditating, or taking my supplements
- Less stress

It wasn't always easy, but being intentional about drawing boundaries and saying no gave me consistently better energy and allowed my body the rest time it needed to start healing. My RA healing journey would've taken much longer if I were running around with my friends constantly. I would've been run ragged and miserable most of the time.

If you're going through something tough in your life right now, answer this: **What do I need to say no to that will result in something better in my life?**

For example:

- Saying no to a social event to prioritize your well-being
- Saying no to a request æthat doesn't align with your values or goals
- Saying no to spending time with people who drain or overwhelm you
- Saying no to someone asking for help when you're already overextended
- Saying no to doom-scrolling on social media when you really need to sleep
- Saying no to the expensive vacation with your friends so you can save your money

Take a look at the box below. In the left column, write three or four things you need to say no to that might result in something *better* in your life. In the right column, write what you're saying yes to instead for each thing you're saying no to.

Things I Need to Say 'No' to:	When I Say 'No' to These Things, What I'm Saying 'Yes' to Instead:

By being intentional about what you're saying no to, you can create room for more fulfilling and productive things in your life—especially when times are tough.

If saying no is hard for you, here's something you can try saying instead: "Here's what I *can* do."

One weekend, I was invited out for dinner and drinks with a group of girlfriends, and I thought to myself, "I'm so exhausted I can barely stand up straight. There's no freaking way I'm going to make it through dinner and drinks." I knew I needed to say no and prioritize my rest. But I also really wanted to see my friends! So, here's what I said: "I'm feeling pretty exhausted after this week, so I'm going to have to say no. I can't make it for dinner and drinks. My RA has been a struggle lately, and I need more downtime than usual. *Here's what I can do:* I have some free time on Sunday afternoon. Do you want to grab a coffee or come hang out at my place?"

It's a subtle shift, but quite powerful. I wasn't saying, "No, I can't come, and I don't want to see you." I was declining the initial invitation, giving a very brief reason why, and proposing *what I could do*. This allowed me to set a boundary and prioritize my well-being while also keeping the door open to spending time together in a way that felt comfortable for me.

Try it next time you say no to someone but want to set your own boundary or set your own parameters in a situation. "Here's what I can do." It's an empowering way to set a boundary on your own terms.

Ask for Help

Why is it so damn hard to ask other people for help? I've always struggled with this, and I know other women do, too. We want to do things for ourselves—to be independent and not rely on anyone else. One of the hardest lessons I learned during my RA journey was that *I couldn't do it alone, and I shouldn't have to.*

As a business owner, coach, and self-proclaimed "get shit done" kinda gal, I was used to handling everything myself. If I needed something done, I'd do it. Boom. Problem to solve? I'm on it. Challenge to overcome? I'd tackle it head-on. I always prided myself on being capable and strong. Asking for help felt like admitting defeat or showing weakness.

But when the RA took over my body, I physically could not do everything for myself anymore. There were days when I couldn't open a jar because my hands hurt so badly. There were mornings it took me 20 minutes to get dressed because my joints were so stiff. There were weeks when I was too exhausted to cook dinner or go grocery shopping. I reached my breaking point and realized that I had no choice but to let people in and ask for help.

And it was one of the most important things I did for myself during that time.

I had to learn that **asking for help is not a sign of weakness**. It's a sign of self-awareness and strength. It takes courage to be vulnerable and admit you can't handle everything on your own. It takes wisdom to recognize you need support. And it takes trust to let other people show up for you.

My husband stepped up in ways I never expected. He cooked the majority of our meals, handled chores around the house, and held me when I cried from the pain and frustration. My friends checked in on me regularly, brought me food, and sat with me on the couch watching movies when I didn't have the energy to go out. My family sent me encouraging texts and called me just to listen. My business coach helped me restructure my workload so I wasn't so overwhelmed.

None of this would've happened if I hadn't let them in. If I kept pretending everything was fine or if I said, "I'm good!" when people asked how I was doing. I had to ask for help when I saw the opportunity.

I see this with a lot of women I coach. They're juggling a million things, going through something incredibly difficult, and yet they are reluctant to ask for help or accept support from others. They don't want to "burden" anyone. They don't want to seem "needy" or "weak." They think they should be able to handle everything themselves.

But there is magic in these four simple words: *I need your help.*

Asking for help doesn't make you weak. I'd argue it makes you stronger. It means you're aware of your limits and boundaries, you're confident enough to show yourself to the world when you're not at your "best," and you are asserting what you need so you can move forward into a better place.

My coaching client, Michelle, hired me to support her during a job search in one of the most challenging job markets in decades. Michelle knew she wanted to find a new job but was struggling with getting an offer after a few months of searching. When she submitted applications, she rarely heard back and felt like her resume was just disappearing into a black hole. When she did finally hear back from one company and had a job interview, they ended up moving forward with someone else. Michelle felt stuck. She didn't know what else to do, but she didn't want to ask anyone else for help. "Why can't I figure this out myself?" she asked herself.

With some encouragement from her husband, Michelle swallowed her pride and decided to hire me as her coach to help her with her job search. Right away, we jumped in and:

- Audited her application materials
- Updated and optimized her LinkedIn profile
- Created a networking strategy to leverage the relationships she'd built throughout her career
- Crafted a compelling elevator pitch for Michelle to tell her "story" during networking conversations and job interviews
- Polished her interview skills so she could really sell herself and her skills

Within two months, Michelle had not one but two job offers from organizations she described as "dream companies." This meant she had the power to negotiate a great offer and ultimately accept the job that felt like the best fit for her.

After accepting her new job, Michelle reflected back to me: "I'm proud of myself for realizing that it's OK to ask for help. After hiring you and getting the support I needed, things shifted almost immediately in my job search. That never would've happened if I kept trying to do it all on my own."

Here are some other examples of what it looks like to ask for help during a tough time:

- Seeking out a financial adviser to help create a plan for paying off debt and saving for the future
- Going to therapy to navigate the emotional aftermath of a divorce or breakup
- Asking your manager for guidance on a work project you're struggling to complete
- Hiring a personal trainer and nutritionist to develop a health plan after a difficult diagnosis
- Talking about your challenges to a compassionate friend who will listen without judgment
- Working with a career coach to guide you after a surprise layoff
- Asking a trusted coworker for advice about navigating a complex team dynamic

Where in your life or career do you need help right now? Whatever it is, you don't have to go at it alone. And you shouldn't have to. In the box below, write one or more areas of your life that would improve if you asked for help:

<table>
<tr><td>Where I Need Help in My Life/Career Right Now:</td></tr>
<tr><td>

</td></tr>
</table>

Like my RA journey and Michelle's job search, asking for help might be one of the most important things you do for yourself. Because just burying your struggles or pretending they don't exist isn't authentic—and it will hold you back from the success you deserve.

Get Your Mojo Back When You're Ready

At some point, the fog will start to lift, and you're going to start feeling like yourself again. It happened to me, and it will happen to you. It probably won't be fast, and it probably won't be all at once, but it **will** happen. You'll wake up one day and smile at yourself in the mirror. Or have a conversation with a friend that feels just plain normal. Or you'll feel yourself being excited or ready for something that hasn't excited you in a while.

And when you start feeling that you're ready, take action and get your mojo back! Don't hesitate or say, "What if I'm not ready...." Get back in the saddle and start finding your joy again.

I remember so clearly when my RA pain started to slowly improve. I would wake up some mornings feeling a little less stiff, a bit more energetic, and not needing as much Advil. All of a sudden I wanted to be more social and see my friends more on the weekends. I had the sudden urge to do home decorating projects, and I even felt like getting back in the gym.

They're small things, but they're the things that helped me get my mojo back. I slowly and intentionally started to get back into the things that made me feel like "me" again:

- I joined a new book club that met once a month.
- I started reaching out to friends to meet up for coffee dates and happy hours—something that I had stopped doing for almost two years.
- I began walking to my office rather than driving.
- I rejoined Orange Theory and started working out for the first time since I was diagnosed with RA and committed to just one class a week while I slowly got back into it.

Getting back to the things I enjoy helped me to create pockets of joy in my week, regain my confidence, and feel authentically "Kate" for the first time in a while.

Be aware of signs that you're ready to take action and find YOUR joy again. Coming out of a dark period can feel like a bit of an emotional hangover. That's normal. You can intentionally and purposefully find the small things that help you get your mojo back when you're ready.

Even when you're struggling, you can still find authentic success.

Life <u>will</u> throw challenges at you. You'll get knocked down and feel defeated. Those moments are the greatest tests of authentic success. Give yourself grace, practice gratitude and recognize your wins, set clear boundaries and say no, ask for help from your support system, and when you're ready, get your mojo back.

Chapter 8 Recap:

1. My rheumatoid arthritis (RA) diagnosis was devastating, causing me to waver in my authentic success mindset. We all have challenging times in our lives that make it difficult to stay true to ourselves through the tough periods.

2. Give yourself grace during these tough times—it is crucial for maintaining your well-being. Acknowledge your struggles without criticizing yourself, and create the space you need for staying true to yourself and healing emotionally.

3. Practice gratitude and recognize your wins. Pick a gratitude practice that is realistic and sustainable for you on a daily basis. Acknowledge your progress and feel proud of yourself.

4. Setting clear boundaries is essential when you're going through something challenging. Ask yourself, "What do I need to say no to that will result in something better in my life?"

5. Asking for help is not a sign of weakness. It's a sign of self-awareness and strength. You can't go through the hard stuff alone, and you

shouldn't have to. Have the courage, wisdom, and trust to let other people help support you.

6. When you're ready, get your mojo back! Get back in the saddle and find your joy again. Because you WILL get to the other side of your adversity, and when you do, you'll want to reemerge and feel like "you" again.

Conclusion

Congrats on making it to the end! By completing this book, you've discovered your core values, upgraded your mindset, identified your unique communication style, and established better habits. You have a strong foundation for networking, mentorship, overcoming challenges, and staying authentic in our AI-driven world.

The concepts in this book don't work if YOU don't do the work. You have a choice:

1. Keep doing what you've always done. Close this book, put it on some shelf where it'll collect dust, and keep living your life the way you have been.

2. Commit to authentic success. Take the lessons you learned in this book and incorporate them into your life and career starting *now*. It doesn't have to be perfect overnight, but commit to getting started. Pick the one to three concepts that resonated with you most and start working on them right away. Keep this book out somewhere you can see it and revisit it periodically to keep you moving forward.

I believe you'll choose option 2. You read this book because you believe in your ability to be authentically successful. You didn't want just another feel-good self-help book. You're ready to achieve your goals and kick some ass – while staying true to yourself and your values.

We've talked about accountability several times in this book. **Accountability really matters.** Remember that the American Society of Training and Development (ASTD) did a study on accountability and found that you have a 65 percent chance of completing a goal if you share your goal with another person. And if you have a specific accountability appointment with a person you've shared your goals with, you will increase your chance of success by up to 95 percent.

If you want additional support or accountability, that's why Shattered Glass Coaching is here. As a Career Coach, I work with ambitious women, coaching them professionally to show up with confidence, take control of their careers, and live with joy, energy, and fulfillment. Coaches are mentors, career supports, goal planners, and sources of accountability and encouragement. We help you create a roadmap to reach your personal and professional goals. Use the QR code below to learn more about working with Shattered Glass Coaching, and to book your FREE introductory coaching call:

Anything you want to achieve, personally or professionally, is possible by being authentically *you*.

Acknowledgements

Writing a book about authentic success meant I had to live it. I couldn't have done that without the people who believed in me, pushed me, and reminded me to keep going.

Adam, you are my biggest supporter and my safe place. You never once doubted that this book would happen, even when I did. Thank you for the pep talks, the patience, and for keeping me fed and caffeinated during writing sessions. I love you 7ever.

Mom and Dad, thank you for raising me to believe I could do anything I set my mind to. You taught me to chase my dreams without apologizing, and that confidence is the foundation of everything I've built. I hope I've made you proud.

Lauren, my first reader ever– you've always known I would write a book. Thank you for being the Christina to my Meredith and for always believing in what I could become.

Jennifer Dawn, thank you for helping me build Shattered Glass Coaching from the ground up. So much of who I am as a coach is because of you. I'm honored to have you open this book.

Douglas Robbins, thank you for helping me get this book off the ground and keeping the momentum going when the blank page felt impossible. Your guidance made all the difference. And to my early readers, Michelle Brown, Bonnie Wims, and Krista Garrett, thank you for your feedback, encouragement, and for making this book better than I could have made it alone.

Jen Schwytzer, thank you for your friendship, your thoughtful feedback, and for always being in my corner. I'm so glad that conference in Dallas brought us together all those years ago.

Stephanie Exner and all the Harvest Goal Collective ladies, thank you for holding me accountable and believing in this book. You helped me stay the course when life got busy and excuses got tempting.

Steve and Susie Baskin, you are the greatest career mentors I've ever had. So much of what I teach my clients today started with what I learned from you. Thank you for seeing my potential and pushing me to rise to it.

Mrs. Goodson, my third-grade teacher– you were the first person to tell me I had a gift for writing. I never forgot that. This book exists because you planted that seed so many years ago.

To Mattie, Laurie, Alyssa, and Britton– thank you for helping me turn a manuscript into a real book. Your expertise and guidance made this process smoother than I ever imagined. I couldn't have done this without your team!

And to Clara and Winston– you two keep me inspired and feeling young. I can't wait to watch you grow up and chase your own versions of authentic success. The world is lucky to have you.

Finally, to my clients, past, present, and future. Your stories fill these pages, and your courage to pursue careers that actually fit who you are inspires me every single day. Thank you for trusting me with your journeys.

Sources[*]

Zillow San Diego: https://www.zillow.com/home-values/54296/ san-diego-ca/

2019 Gallup poll: "Americans' Perceptions of Success in the U.S.":

https://news.gallup.com/opinion/gallup/266927/americans-percep-tions-success.aspx

Carol Dweck, *Mindset: The New Psychology of Success*:

https://www.elliottbaybook.com/item/XTKcqJIK5P-ovCNBHQ_k8A

Nature Communications thoughts research: https://www.nature.com/ articles/s41467-020-17255-9

Positive Psychology – CBT Psychologists on Thought Journaling: "What Is a Thought Diary in CBT? 5 Templates and Examples":

https://positivepsychology.com/thought-diary/

Atomic Habits by James Clear: https://jamesclear.com/atomic-habits

Research by the Society for Personality and Social Psychology on Habit Creation: "How We Form Habits and Change Existing Ones":

https://spsp.org/news-center/press-release/how-we-form-habits-and-change-existing-ones#:~:text=Much%20of%20our%20daily%20 lives,on%20the%20goal%20or%20outcome.

James Clear's Habit Tracker from *Atomic Habits*: https://jamesclear. com/habit-tracker

Research on Habits by Dr. Jeremy Dean: "How Long To Form A Habit? 66 Days Is A Rough Average:

https://www.spring.org.uk/2024/11/form-habit-66.php

Charles Duhigg, *The Power of Habit*: https://charlesduhigg.com/the-power-of-habit/

The American Society of Training and Development (ASTD) study on accountability: *ASTD Handbook of Measuring and Evaluating Training:*

https://books.google.com/books?hl=en&lr=&id=m-HTEkvyjaLwC&oi=fnd&pg=PR1&dq=astd+study+on+accountability&ots=Tl_zG176Yi&sig=qGr1ndwsihxE_Pd2ko0WhPtsuJk#v=onepage&q=astd%20study%20on%20accountability&f=false

Gallup research on personal AI usage: "AI Use at Work Has Nearly Doubled in Two Years":

https://www.gallup.com/workplace/691643/work-nearly-doubled-two-years.aspx#:~:text=White%2DCollar%20Workers%20Regularly%20Use,once%20per%20year%2C%20or%20never?&text=Line%20graph%20showing%20that%20from,(11%25%20to%209%25).&text=Frequent%20AI%20use%20is%20also,AI%20will%20eliminate%20their%20job.

Stanford's 2025 AI Index Report: "The 2025 AI Index Report": https://hai.stanford.edu/ai-index/2025-ai-index-report

SQ Magazine Report on AI-generated content on social media: "AI in Social Media Tools Statistics 2025: Uncover What's Shaping the Future": https://sqmagazine.co.uk/ai-in-social-media-tools-statistics/#:~:text=AI%E2%80%91Generated%20Content%20Statistics,Media%20Demographics%20Influenced%20by%20AI

BMC Health Service Research about authentic communication: "Quality communication can improve patient-centred health outcomes among older patients: a rapid review":

https://bmchealthservres.biomedcentral.com/articles/10.1186/s12913-023-09869-8

Forbes article on the power of vulnerability in leadership: "The Power Of Vulnerability In Leadership: Experts Say Authenticity And Honesty Can Move People And Achieve Results":

https://www.forbes.com/sites/luisromero/2023/03/08/the-power-of-vulnerability-in-leadership-experts-say-authenticity-and-honesty-can-move-people-and-achieve-results/

Tech Layoffs 2025: "Tech Layoffs 2025: Why AI is Behind the Rising Job Cuts": https://www.finalroundai.com/blog/ai-tech-layoffs-mid-2025#:~:text=roles%20disappearing%20first-,1.,Data%20analysis

True Up layoff tracker: "Tech Layoffs Tracker": https://www.trueup.io/layoffs

Mashable news article about Fiverr layoffs: "Fiverr to cut 30 percent of workforce in AI pivot": https://mashable.com/article/fiverr-layoffs-ai-pivot?test_uuid=04wb5avZVbBe1OWK6996faM&test_variant=b#:~:text=Fiverr%2C%20the%20online%20freelance%20gig%20marketplace%2C%20is,about%2030%20percent%20of%20the%20Fiverr%20workforce.

Pavilion article about failed AI initiatives: "Why 85% of AI Projects Are Expensive Failures": https://www.joinpavilion.com/blog/why-85-of-ai-projects-are-expensive-failures#:~:text=We%27ve%20never%20seen%20technology,age%20of%20the%201970s%2D1990s.

A study on social networks conducted by researchers at Columbia University and the University of Wisconsin-Madison:

https://sites.stat.columbia.edu/gelman/research/published/DiPreteetal.pdf

Research by Susan Cain in *Quiet: The Power of Introverts in a World That Can't Stop Talking*: https://susancain.net/book/quiet/

2019 CNBC/SurveyMonkey: "Work Survey and Workplace Happiness Index":

https://www.surveymonkey.com/newsroom/cnbc-and-surveymonkey-release-latest-quarterly-work-survey-and-workplace-happiness-index/

Catalyst study: "The facts about gender representation": https://www.catalyst.org/en-us/insights/featured/gender-representation

Women Ahead Study about mentorship: "The Impact Of Mentorship On Employee Empowerment":

https://www.forbes.com/councils/forbeshumanresourcescouncil/2024/05/15/the-impact-of-mentorship-on-employee-empowerment/

2019 study by Olivet Nazarene University on mentorship: "Study explores professional mentor-mentee relationships in 2019":

https://web.archive.org/web/20220405012135/https://online.olivet.edu/research-statistics-on-professional-mentors

Wharton Study about the value of being a mentor: "Workplace Loyalties Change, but the Value of Mentoring Doesn't":

https://knowledge.wharton.upenn.edu/podcast/knowledge-at-wharton-podcast/workplace-loyalties-change-but-the-value-of-mentoring-doesnt/

AnitaB study on women in tech: https://legacy.anitab.org/blog/events/ghc/empowering-the-future-of-tech-bridging-the-gender-gap/

2022 Carson Group study on women in financial services: "2022 Women in Wealth Management Report":

https://www.carsongroup.com/women-in-wealth-report-2022/

Pew Research Center poll on women in leadership: "Women in Leadership 2018": https://www.pewsocialtrends.org/wp-content/uploads/sites/3/2018/09/Gender-and-leadership-FULL-REPORT2.pdf

The Grateful Brain by neuroscientist, Dr. Alex Korb: https://www.psychologytoday.com/us/blog/prefrontal-nudity/201211/the-grateful-brain

Psychology Today article about people-pleasing: "People-Pleasing":

https://www.psychologytoday.com/us/basics/people-pleasing

*At the time of publication, all links were current and working.